Thanks for bringing **VICTORY** back home to the **MOTOR CITY!**

1.866.STAY.MCC • motorcitycasino.com

MotorCity Casino Hotel and MotorCity Casino Hotel design are trademarks of Detroit Entertainment, L.L.C. ©2008 Detroit Entertainment, L.L.C. All rights reserved.

If you bet more than you can afford to lose, you've got a problem. Call 1-800-270-7117 for free, confidential help.

Copyright © 2008 Detroit Red Wings Hockey Club

All Rights Reserved. No part of this book may be reproduced, stored in a retrieval system or transmitted, in any form by any means, electronically, mechanically, photocopying or otherwise, without the prior written permission from the publisher, Detroit Red Wings, 19 Steve Yzerman Drive, Detroit, Michigan 48226.

Director: Michael Bayoff

Managing Editor: Bill Roose

Photo Editor: Bill Roose

Copy Editor: Bill Roose

Writers: Michael Caples, Kevin Fitzhenry, Derek Gluth, Bill Roose, Lindsey Ungar

Creative Design: Craig C. Wheeler, CFW Creative Sports, Inc.

Produced by: CFW Creative Sports, Inc.

Special thanks: Archivist Sharon Arend, Ilitch Holdings; Craig Campbell, Hockey Hall of Fame; Alexandre Harvey, Montreal Canadiens; Gavin Smith Photography; Getty Images photographers Dave Reginek, Tom Turrill, Dave Sandford, Gregory Shamus, Jeff Vinnick, Bill Wippert, John Russell, Michael Martin, Chris Graythen, Doug Pensinger, Christian Petersen, Glenn James, Ronald Martinez, Bruce Bennett, Jim McIsaac and Claus Andersen.

Library of Congress Control Number: 2008930059

ISBN: 0-9817729-1-9

ISBN 13: 978-0-9817729-1-2

Printed in the United States

Copyright © the Detroit Red Wings Hockey Club and the Winged Wheel. All rights reserved.

CONTENTS

How the Wings were built	6
The Team	8
The Season	28
The Past	50
The All-Stars	72
The Playoffs	74
Tentacle Tradition	88
Father Fan	100
The Cup	114

DETROIT RED WINGS
Owner/Governor MIKE ILITCH
Owner/Secretary-Treasurer MARIAN ILITCH
Vice President/Alternate Governor CHRISTOPHER ILITCH
Senior Vice President/Alternate Governor JIM DEVELLANO
Executive Vice President/General Manager/Alternate Governor KEN HOLLAND
Vice President/Alternate Governor STEVE YZERMAN
General Counsel/Alternate Governor ROBERT E. CARR
Senior Vice President of Business Affairs STEVE VIOLETTA
Vice President/Assistant General Manager JIM NILL
Vice President of Finance PAUL MACDONALD
Head Coach MIKE BABCOCK
Associate Coaches PAUL MACLEAN & TODD MCLELLAN
Goaltending Coach JIM BEDARD
Video Coach JAY WOODCROFT
Director of Hockey Administration RYAN MARTIN
Consultant SCOTTY BOWMAN
Director of Pro Scouting MARK HOWE
Pro Scouts PAT VERBEEK, BOB MCCAMMON, GLENN MERKOSKY
Director of Amateur Scouting JOE MCDONNELL
Amateur Scouts BRUCE HARALSON, DAVID KOLB, MARK LEACH
Director of European Scouting HAKAN ANDERSSON
European Scouts VLADIMIR HAVLUJ, EVGENI ERFILOV, ARI VOURI
Part-Time Scout MARTY STEIN
Executive Assistants KATHI WYATT, LAUREN STOTT
Accounting Assistant BRIDGET MERRITT
Athletic Therapist PIET VAN ZANT
Assistant Athletic Therapist RUSS BAUMANN
Equipment Manager PAUL BOYER
Assistant Equipment Manager CHRIS SCOPPETTO
Team Masseur SERGEI TCHEKMAREV
Medical Director DONALD W. WEAVER, MD
Team Physicians ANTHONY COLUCCI, DO; DOUGLAS G. PLAGENS, MD
Team Dentist C.J. REGULA, DMD
Senior Director of Communications JOHN HAHN
Community Relations Manager ANNE MARIE KRAPPMANN
Media Relations Manager TODD BEAM
Media Relations Coordinator LISA HICKOK
Community Relations Coordinator KELLI KEARLY
Director of Advertising Sales KURT BUHLER
Account Executives MARY GREENER, MARK KELLY, DOUG MURPHY
Account Service Manager NICOLE CHAMBERS
Director of Marketing/Promotions LORI SHIELS
Executive Producer, Event Entertainment AYRON SEQUEIRA
Marketing Coordinator JIM BIEWER
Marketing Assistant KIMBERLY PALTER
Youth Hockey Manager, Fan Development PHIL PIERCE
Director of Ticket Sales & Service JOE BARBER
Ticket Service & Retention Manager MOLLY WURDACK
Group Sales Manager KRISTIN OUIMET
Season Ticket Coordinator CHAD WARDIE
Season Ticket Account Executives CHAD PAINTER, JOE SMITH, ERICH FREINY, BRIDGET HIGGS, KEVIN LAO
Director of New Media, Publishing Alimni Relations MIKE BAYOFF
New Media & Publishing Manager BILL ROOSE
Web Video Manager RYAN DOHERTY
Director of Broadcasting SHELDON NUEMAN
Radio Broadcasters KEN KAL, PAUL WOODS
TV Broadcasters KEN DANIELS, MICKEY REDMOND, LARRY MURPHY

JOE LOUIS ARENA
President DANA WARG
Vice President/General Manager TIM PADGETT
Vice President, Sales & Marketing BILL LEE
Vice President, Hospitality, Catering & Restaurant Operations MICHAEL PRAINITO
Vice President, Corporate Security/Parking Services RICHARD FENTON
Vice President of Finance LARRY SILVER
Director/General Manager, Hockeytown Café STEVE DAVIDSON
Director of Finance KEITH DOWDICAN
Director of Building Operations JAMES BULLO
Director of Hospitality MIKE BEREND
Director of Suites Sales & Administration KIMBERLY RECKLEY
Director of Corporate Security & Safety JOHNNY JACKSON
Director of Creative Services MICHELLE CHMURA
Director of Merchandise JENNIFER TRACY

Produced by
CFW
CREATIVE SPORTS INC.
2955 Riverside Drive • Trenton, MI 48183
734 561-6100 • cfwcreativesports.com

HOW THE WINGS WERE BUILT

NO.	POS	NAME	HOW ACQUIRED
30	G	Chris Osgood	Signed as a free agent, August 8, 2005; originally drafted by Red Wings in 1991 (third choice, 54th overall)
35	G	Jimmy Howard	Drafted by Red Wings in 2003 (second choice, 64th overall)
39	G	Dominik Hasek	Signed as a free agent, July 31, 2006
3	D	Andreas Lilja	Signed as free agent, August 24, 2005
4	D	Kyle Quincy	Drafted by Red Wings in 2003 (fourth choice, 132nd overall)
5	D	Nicklas Lidstrom	Drafted by Red Wings in 1989 (third choice, 53rd overall)
8	LW	Justin Abdelkader	Drafted by Red Wings in 2005 (second choice, 42nd overall)
11	RW	Dan Cleary	Signed as free agent, October 4, 2005
13	C	Pavel Datsyuk	Drafted by Red Wings in 1998 (sixth choice, 171st overall)
14	D	Derek Meech	Drafted by Red Wings in 2002 (seventh choice, 229th overall)
17	RW	Dallas Drake	Signed as a free agent, July 9, 2007; originally drafted by Wings in 1898 (sixth choice, 116th overall)
18	LW	Kirk Maltby	Obtained from Edmonton for Dan McGillis, March 20, 1996
20	RW	Aaron Downey	Signed as a free agent, October 3, 2007
22	D	Brett Lebda	Signed as a free agent, July 21, 2004
23	D	Brad Stuart	Acquired from Los Angeles February 26, 2008 in exhange for 2009 second and fourth-round draft choices
24	D	Chris Chelios	Acquired from Chicago March 23, 1999 in exchange for Andres Eriksson and two first round draft picks
25	RW	Darrren McCarty	Signed as a free agent, February 25, 2008; originally drafted by Wings in 1992 (second choice, 46th overall)
26	RW	Jiri Hudler	Drafted by Red Wings in 2002 (second choice, 58th overall)
28	D	Brian Rafalski	Signed as a free agent, July 1, 2007
33	C	Kris Draper	Obtained from Winnipeg for future considerations, June 30, 1993
37	RW	Mikael Samuelsson	Signed as a free agent, September 17, 2005
40	LW	Henrik Zetterberg	Drafted by Red Wings in 1999 (seventh choice, 210th overall)
42	C	Mattias Ritola	Drafted by Red Wings in 2005 (fourth choice, 103rd overall)
43	C	Darren Helm	Drafted by Red Wings in 2005 (fifth choice, 132nd overall)
44	C	Mark Hartigan	Signed as an unrestricted free agent, July 2007
46	D	Jakub Kindl	Drafted by Red Wings in 2005 (first selection, 19th overall)
51	C	Valtteri Filppula	Drafted by Red Wings in 2002 (third choice, 95th overall)
52	D	Jonathan Ericsson	Drafted by Red Wings in 2002 (ninth choice, 291st overall)
55	D	Nicklas Kronwall	Drafted by Red Wings in 2000 (first choice, 29th overall)
82	RW	Tomas Kopecky	Drafted by Red Wings in 2000 (second choice, 38th overall)
93	C	Johan Franzen	Drafted by Red Wings in 2004 (third choice, 97th overall)
96	RW	Tomas Holmstrom	Drafted by Red Wings in 1994 (10th choice, 257th overall)

2007-08 STANLEY CUP CHAMPIONS

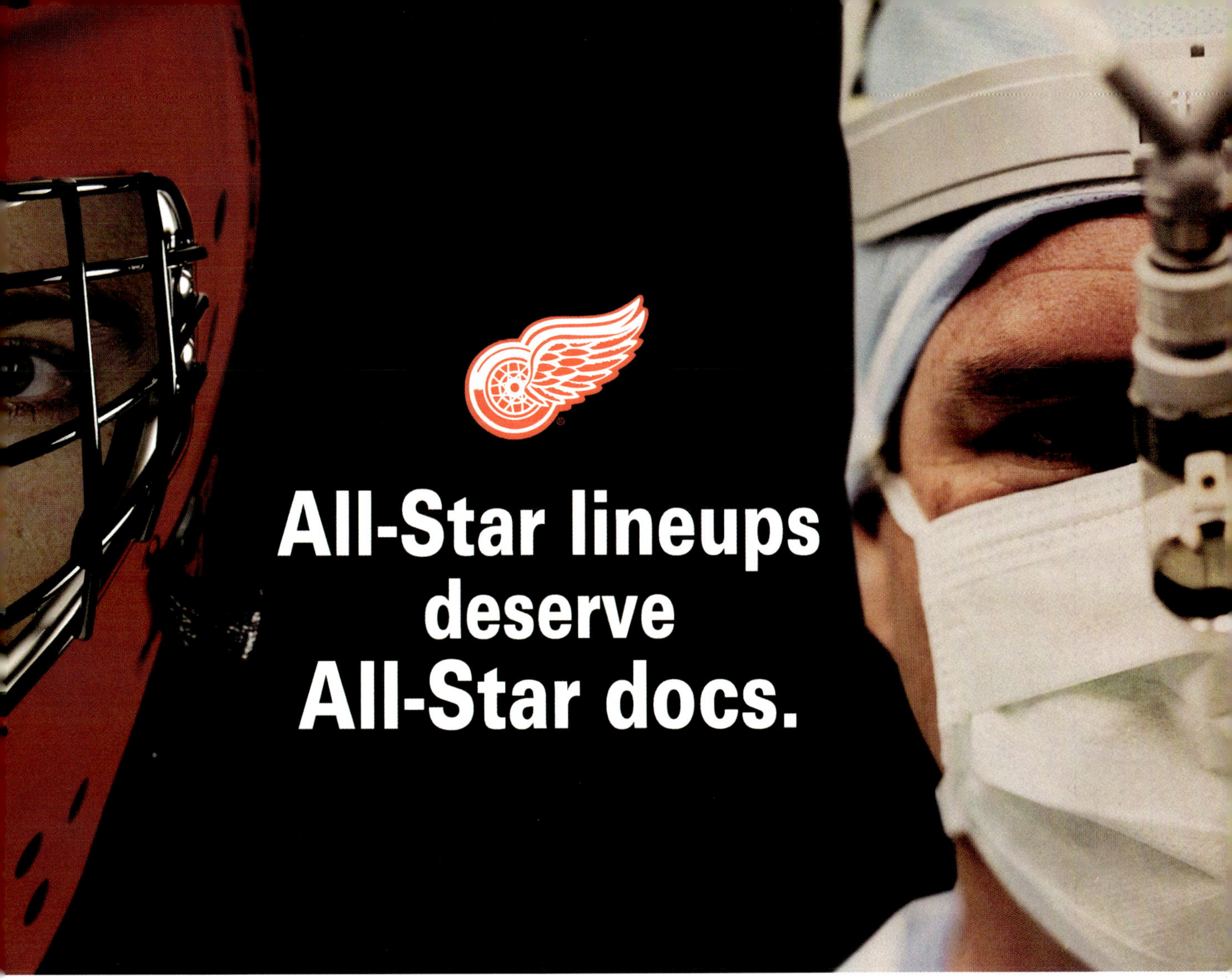

All-Star lineups deserve All-Star docs.

Congratulations on another incredible season!

We're proud to be the team behind the team.

DETROIT MEDICAL CENTER

For your All-Star Sports Medicine Doc, call 1-888-DMC-2500 or visit DMC.org.

Detroit Medical Center - Official Healthcare Services Provider of the Detroit Red Wings.

With comments by Ken Holland

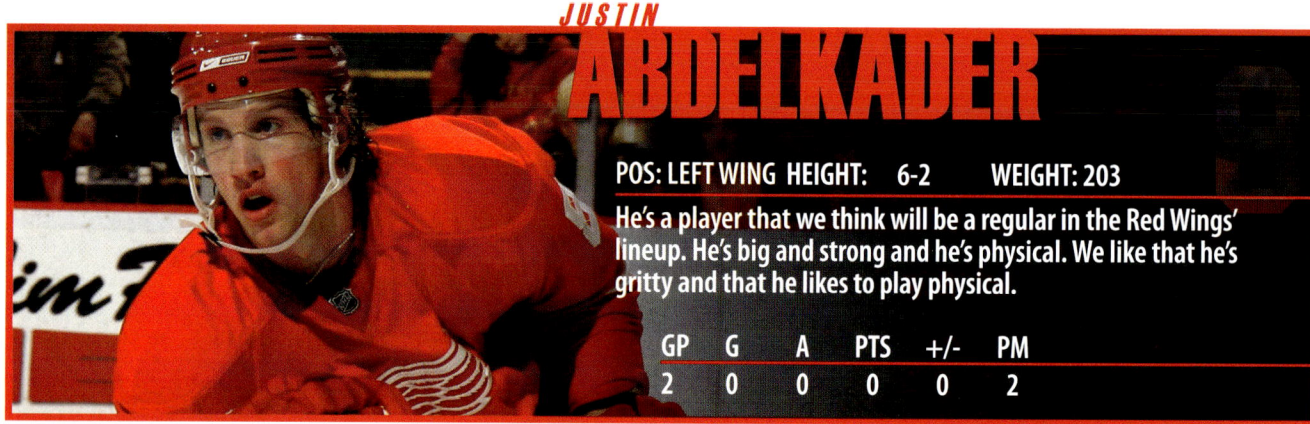

JUSTIN ABDELKADER

POS: LEFT WING **HEIGHT:** 6-2 **WEIGHT:** 203

He's a player that we think will be a regular in the Red Wings' lineup. He's big and strong and he's physical. We like that he's gritty and that he likes to play physical.

GP	G	A	PTS	+/-	PM
2	0	0	0	0	2

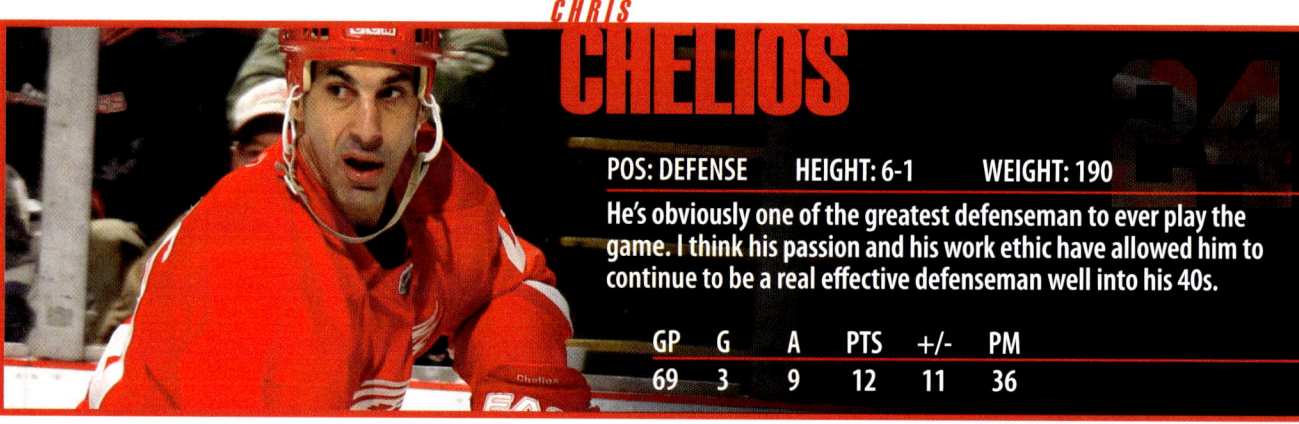

CHRIS CHELIOS

POS: DEFENSE **HEIGHT:** 6-1 **WEIGHT:** 190

He's obviously one of the greatest defenseman to ever play the game. I think his passion and his work ethic have allowed him to continue to be a real effective defenseman well into his 40s.

GP	G	A	PTS	+/-	PM
69	3	9	12	11	36

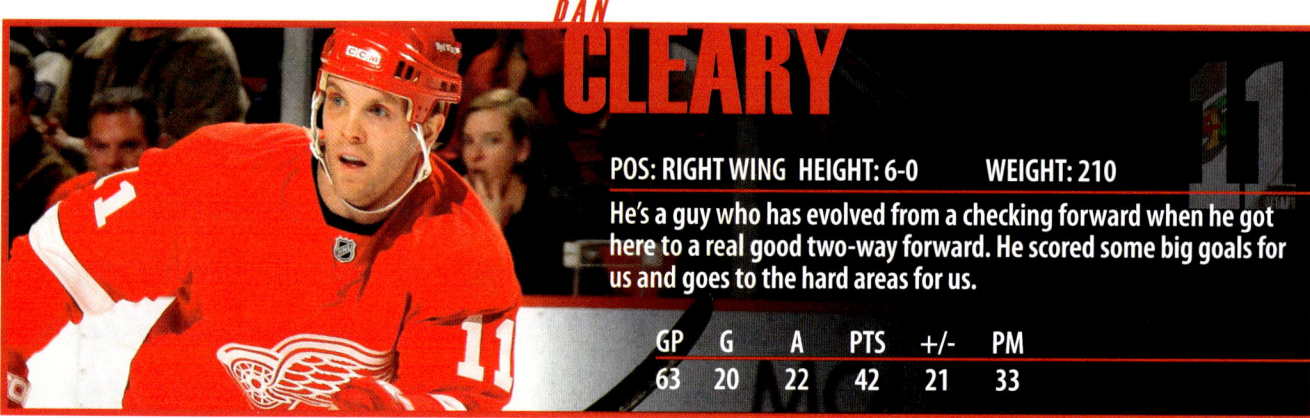

DAN CLEARY

POS: RIGHT WING **HEIGHT:** 6-0 **WEIGHT:** 210

He's a guy who has evolved from a checking forward when he got here to a real good two-way forward. He scored some big goals for us and goes to the hard areas for us.

GP	G	A	PTS	+/-	PM
63	20	22	42	21	33

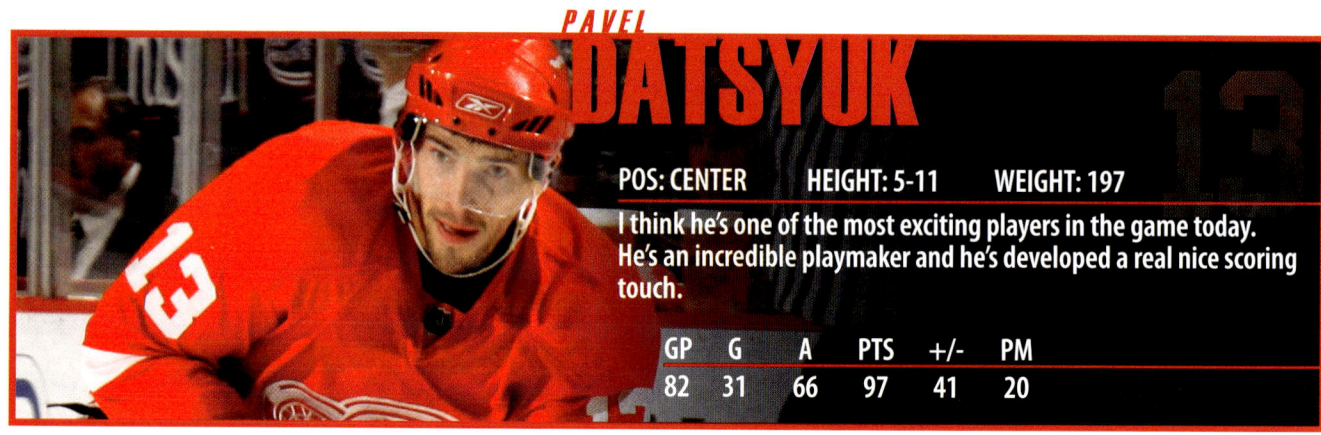

PAVEL DATSYUK

POS: CENTER **HEIGHT:** 5-11 **WEIGHT:** 197

I think he's one of the most exciting players in the game today. He's an incredible playmaker and he's developed a real nice scoring touch.

GP	G	A	PTS	+/-	PM
82	31	66	97	41	20

ASPEN

PACIFICA

300

SEBRING SEDAN

SEBRING CONVERTIBLE

THE ALL-NEW TOWN & COUNTRY

GO RED WINGS!

SEE YOUR CHRYSLER AND JEEP® SUPERSTORES

WWW.CHRYSLERJEEPSUPERSTORES.COM

Chrysler is a registered trademark of Chrysler LLC.

AARON DOWNEY

POS: RIGHT WING **HEIGHT:** 6-0 **WEIGHT:** 216

He did a tremendous job all year for us standing up for his teammates doing all of the dirty work. He's positive; hard working.

GP	G	A	PTS	+/-	PM
56	0	3	3	0	116

DALLAS DRAKE

POS: RIGHT WING **HEIGHT:** 6-0 **WEIGHT:** 192

Character and grit. He's just a guy who brings a lot of ingredients and likes to play physical. He did a real good job on the penalty kill for us.

GP	G	A	PTS	+/-	PM
65	3	3	6	-12	41

KRIS DRAPER

POS: CENTER **HEIGHT:** 5-10 **WEIGHT:** 190

He brings a tremendous amount of passion, energy, speed to our lineup. He's a real good penalty-killer and a real good leader for us on and off the ice.

GP	G	A	PTS	+/-	PM
65	9	8	17	-2	68

JONATHAN ERICSSON

POS: DEFENSE **HEIGHT:** 6-5 **WEIGHT:** 205

He's a guy that we think can play regularly for us down the road. He was a forward and learned to play defense. He has a lot of upside and we're very optimistic and high on him.

GP	G	A	PTS	+/-	PM
8	1	0	1	-3	4

Built for Entertainment.

With hockey season almost over, we've got your entertainment needs covered. This Spring, Casino Windsor will become Caesars Windsor, showcasing many of the world's biggest names in entertainment in our new 5,000 seat entertainment center. Visit caesarswindsor.com for details, and say goodbye to post-season blues.

tickets available at caesarswindsor.com

Know Your Limit, Play Within It! All ages welcome in our Augustus Tower and convention complex. Must be 19 years of age or older to enter the casino and all other outlets.

VALTTERI FILPPULA — 51

POS: CENTER **HEIGHT:** 6-0 **WEIGHT:** 189

He's a real good two-way player with great speed, who can really protect the puck down low. He's a good playmaker and moving forward we hope that he eventually develops more of a scoring touch.

GP	G	A	PTS	+/-	PM
78	19	17	36	16	28

JOHAN FRANZEN — 93

POS: CENTER **HEIGHT:** 6-3 **WEIGHT:** 218

Obviously, the last month of the season and the first two rounds of the playoffs, he really showed that he has the potential to be a power forward. Certainly we think he's a guy who can score 20-25 goals each year and play in all situations.

GP	G	A	PTS	+/-	PM
72	27	11	38	12	51

MARK HARTIGAN — 44

POS: CENTER **HEIGHT:** 6-0 **WEIGHT:** 198

A real good depth player for us. He was a really good top-level player in the AHL. He can play center and he can play left wing. He gave us real good depth.

GP	G	A	PTS	+/-	PM
23	3	1	4	-2	16

DOMINIK HASEK — 39

POS: GOALIE **HEIGHT:** 5-11 **WEIGHT:** 177

Dom played a significant role with us in the regular-season. He's certainly one of the best goalies of his time.

GP	AVG	W-L-OT	SO	GA
41	2.14	27-10-3	5	84

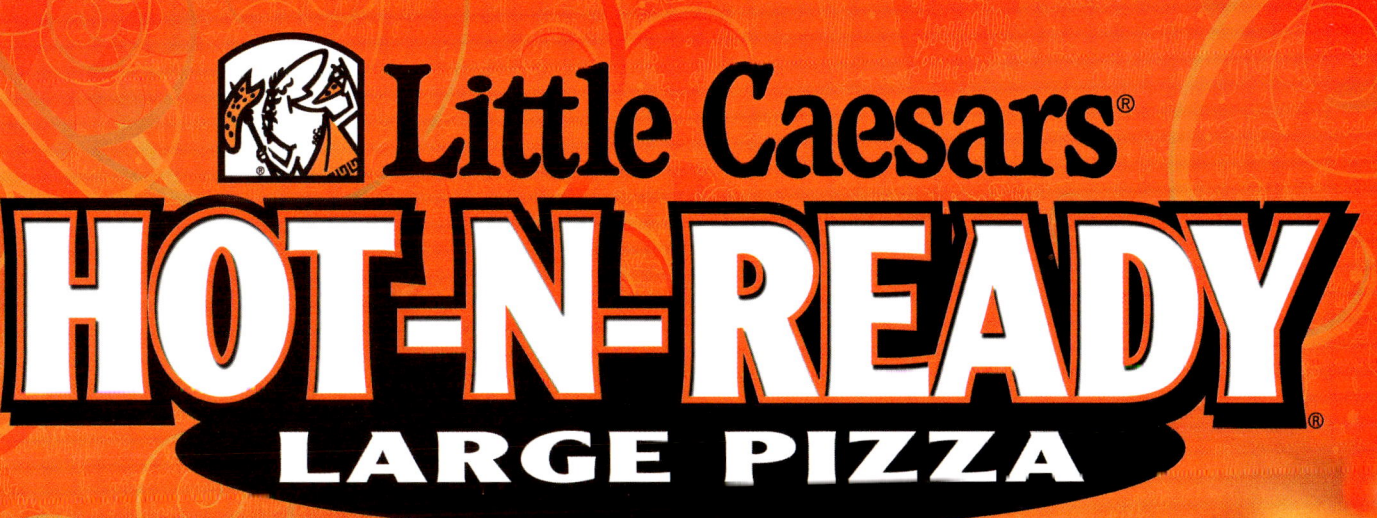

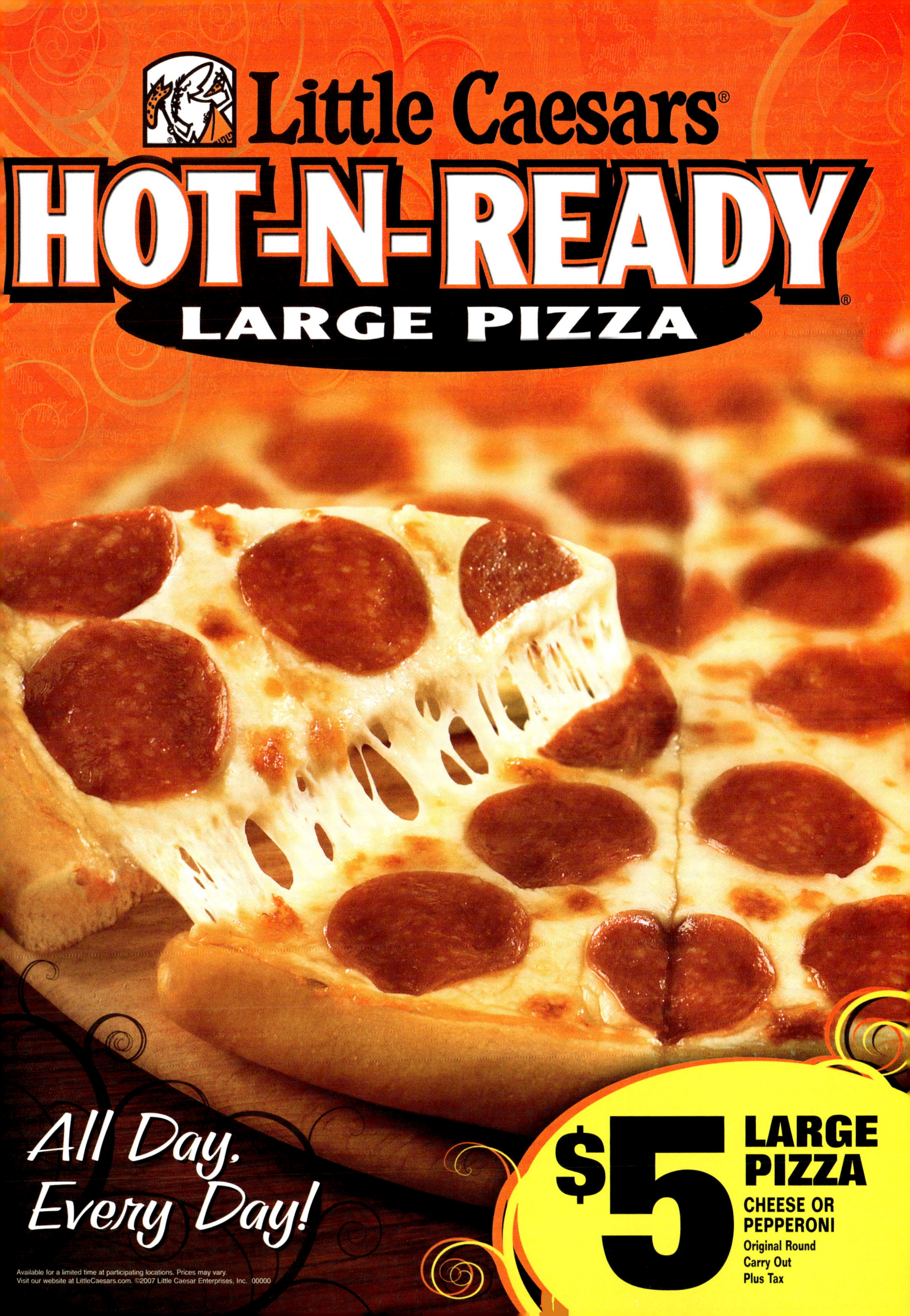
Little Caesars®
HOT-N-READY®
LARGE PIZZA
All Day, Every Day!
$5 LARGE PIZZA
CHEESE OR PEPPERONI
Original Round
Carry Out
Plus Tax
Available for a limited time at participating locations. Prices may vary.
Visit our website at LittleCaesars.com. ©2007 Little Caesar Enterprises, Inc. 00000

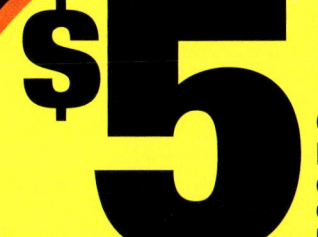

DARREN HELM

43

POS: CENTER HEIGHT: 6-0 WEIGHT: 182

A young player who was probably well ahead of where we thought he would be. He has great speed and he's a good two-way player. He slowly gained the coaches' confidence and began to play a bigger role.

GP	G	A	PTS	+/-	PM
7	0	0	0	-2	2

TOMAS HOLMSTROM

96

POS: RIGHT WING HEIGHT: 6-0 WEIGHT: 202

I think he's the best in the business at what he does. He's the best net-front player in the National Hockey League today because of his ability to take the abuse, but at the same time have the eye-hand coordination to knock pucks out of the air.

GP	G	A	PTS	+/-	PM
59	20	20	40	9	58

JIMMY HOWARD

35

POS: GOALIE HEIGHT: 6-1 WEIGHT: 204

He's a good prospect who had a real good year this year. We think he has the potential to be an NHL goaltender into training camp of '08-09. Next year is s big year for him.

GP	AVG	W-L-OT	SO	GA
4	2.13	0-2-0	0	7

JIRI HUDLER

POS: RIGHT WING HEIGHT: 5-9 WEIGHT: 178

He loves the big games. He has ice in his veins. He's tremendous at protecting the puck down low in the offensive zone. He didn't play a lot of minutes, but in the minutes that he did play he was a big factor for us.

GP	G	A	PTS	+/-	PM
81	13	29	42	11	26

Save the Date!

CELEBRITY GOLF CLASSIC
OAKLAND HILLS · AUGUST 25, 2008

ursomes include: Round of Golf with a Celebrity Guest • Pre-Golf Breakfast • Lunch on the Course
Post-Golf Reception and Awards Presentation • Commemorative Team Photo • Gift Package

A variety of sponsorship opportunities are available. Visit IlitchCharities.org for more information or call (313) 983-6340.

Sunday Soiree
MotorCity Casino Hotel
Sunday, August 24, 2008

Includes:
Exclusive Access to Celebrity Guests
Live Entertainment
Unique Live and Silent Auction Items
Strolling Supper and Cocktails

nting Sponsors:

TOMAS KOPECKY

POS: RIGHT WING **HEIGHT:** 6-3 **WEIGHT:** 200

He had a real good regular-season. He's developing into what we think will be a real good third-line player. He has some size and is physical. We're hoping that he can be a 10-15 goal scorer.

GP	G	A	PTS	+/-	PM
77	5	7	12	2	43

NIKLAS KRONWALL

POS: DEFENSE **HEIGHT:** 6-0 **WEIGHT:** 189

I think this year was a real breakout year for him. Obviously, he was able to stay healthy. He's a tremendous competitor with great skills and as good of an open-ice body-checking there is in the game today.

GP	G	A	PTS	+/-	PM
65	7	28	35	25	44

BRETT LEBDA

POS: DEFENSE **HEIGHT:** 5-9 **WEIGHT:** 194

He's very valuable for us because of his ability to skate the puck out of our zone. He has the ability to join the rush. He's a good guy for us in the third period because he brings speed.

GP	G	A	PTS	+/-	PM
78	3	11	14	-1	48

NICKLAS LIDSTROM

POS: DEFENSE **HEIGHT:** 6-1 **WEIGHT:** 193

He's one of three people who realy drive our team. I think he's been the best defenseman in the game for the last decade. He's our leader, he's our captain and he's the best in the business.

GP	G	A	PTS	+/-	PM
76	10	60	70	40	40

ANDREAS LILJA

POS: DEFENSE **HEIGHT:** 6-3 **WEIGHT:** 230

We like him because he's a real good penalty-killer. He brings size to the back end. He's a real positive guy; very popular with his teammates, and he gives us real good depth.

GP	G	A	PTS	+/-	PM
79	2	10	12	-2	93

KIRK MALTBY

POS: LEFT WING **HEIGHT:** 6-0 **WEIGHT:** 196

He brings energy, is a real good penalty-killer and a very good checker. He's a character guy who never complains.

GP	G	A	PTS	+/-	PM
61	6	4	10	-8	32

DARREN McCARTY

POS: RIGHT WING **HEIGHT:** 6-1 **WEIGHT:** 210

He's a guy who basically was out of hockey. We had no idea with a few games left in the season what he could bring, but he did a nice job of giving us a different dimension on the fourth line.

GP	G	A	PTS	+/-	PM
3	0	1	1	2	2

DEREK MEECH

POS: DEFENSE **HEIGHT:** 5-11 **WEIGHT:** 197

He plays hard and got an opportunity in February when we had a lot of injuries. He played left wing for us in March when we had injuries up front. He has tremendous character.

GP	G	A	PTS	+/-	PM
32	0	3	3	-5	6

COMERICA BANK LEGENDS CLUB
INCLUDES A GOURMET DINNER AND DESSERT BUFFET WITH EVERY TICKET

Watch the playoffs from the Comerica Bank Legends Club.
The club provides all the luxuries of a Suite in one single seat.

Amenities with each Legends Club ticket include:

- Luxury seating designed for your comfort along with a drink holder
- Lavish, all-inclusive buffet with select complimentary beverages
- Olympia Club Game Day Access
- Press notes, team lineups, and statistics
- 14 Flat Panel televisions
- Private restrooms

Playoff Tickets start at $155 each
CALL NOW - LIMITED AVAILABILITY!

20 and 40 person "all-inclusive" Suite Rentals also available starting at $4000

FOR MORE INFORMATION:
313-396-7476

Visit DetroitRedWings.com-Tickets-Executive Suites page for a Virtual Tour of the Legends Club.

CHRIS OSGOOD

POS: GOALIE **HEIGHT:** 5-10 **WEIGHT:** 176

He was a key player in us getting to the finals and winning the Stanley Cup. He played great for us in the regular-season and when he got in there he played the best hockey of his career.

GP	AVG	W-L-OT	SO	GA
43	2.09	27-9-4	4	84

KYLE QUINCEY

POS: DEFENSE **HEIGHT:** 6-1 **WEIGHT:** 207

He's got grit, and we have hopes for him moving forward. We see him as more of a defensive defenseman. We're happy with where his career is going and he's moving in the right direction.

GP	G	A	PTS	+/-	PM
6	0	0	0	-3	4

BRIAN RAFALSKI

POS: DEFENSE **HEIGHT:** 5-10 **WEIGHT:** 200

He's underrated. He's a real good world-class defenseman. We signed him and he did better than we thought. He's the best in the world at going back under pressure and avoiding the rush.

GP	G	A	PTS	+/-	PM
73	13	42	55	27	34

MATTIAS RITOLA

POS: CENTER **HEIGHT:** 6-0 **WEIGHT:** 192

I like his skill level. He has to work on bringing it mentally every game. We like his hockey-sense and we like his strength. I would like to see him have a breakout year in the American League.

GP	G	A	PTS	+/-	PM
2	0	1	1	0	0

MIKAEL SAMUELSSON — 37

POS: RIGHT WING **HEIGHT:** 6-2 **WEIGHT:** 210

He's a versatile guy for us, who played the second point on the power play. He has a tremendous shot and plays puck-possession, which is what we like in our system.

GP	G	A	PTS	+/-	PM
73	11	29	40	21	26

GARRETT STAFFORD — 36

POS: DEFENSE **HEIGHT:** 6-0 **WEIGHT:** 195

He was a real good puck-moving defenseman in the American League. At the NHL level, he's a smooth skater, who can handle the puck, move the puck. He's a real good depth defenseman.

GP	G	A	PTS	+/-	PM
2	0	0	0	0	0

BRAD STUART — 23

POS: DEFENSE **HEIGHT:** 6-2 **WEIGHT:** 213

Stuey was a perfect fit for us. He developed tremendous chemistry with Niklas Kronwall. He's basically a real good defensive defenseman, who likes to play physical.

GP	G	A	PTS	+/-	PM
9	1	1	2	6	2

HENRIK ZETTERBERG — 40

POS: LEFT WING **HEIGHT:** 5-11 **WEIGHT:** 195

I think he's the best two-way player in the game today. He has incredible will and determination. He rose to the occasion in big games in every series. He's a superstar, who comes up with the big play, the big goal.

GP	G	A	PTS	+/-	PM
75	43	49	92	30	34

6 Series

Audi Q7

Cooper S

30 eitel dahm years 1975-2005

Danke Schön
Eitel Dahm wishes to thank his customers for 30 years of BMW business

Front, Eitel, left, Regina and right, Helga Dahm

Bavarian BMW
45550 Dequindre Rd.
Shelby Twp., MI 48317
248.997.7700
www.bavarianmotorvillage.com

Bavarian Motor Village
24717 Gratiot Ave.
Eastpointe, MI 48021
586.772.8600
www.bavarianmotorvillage.com

Serving the Pointes for 30 Years

Audi of Rochester Hills
45441 Dequindre Rd.
Rochester Hills, MI 48307
248.997.7400
www.audiofrochesterhills.com

Motor City Mini
45550 Dequindre Rd.
Shelby Twp., MI 48317
248.997.7700
www.motorcitymini.com

THREE GREAT BRANDS, ONE STANDARD OF EXCELLENCE

DETROIT RED WINGS

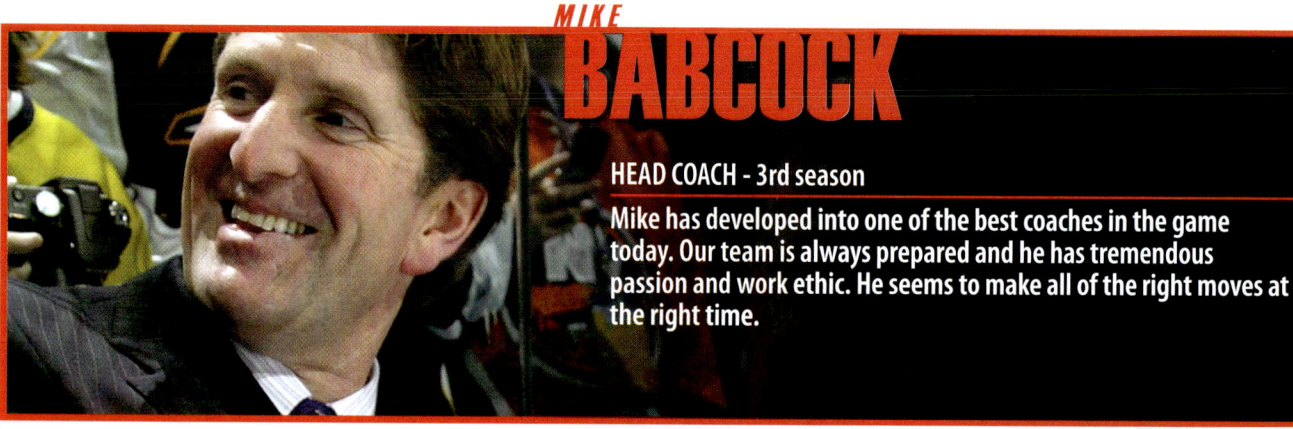

MIKE BABCOCK

HEAD COACH - 3rd season

Mike has developed into one of the best coaches in the game today. Our team is always prepared and he has tremendous passion and work ethic. He seems to make all of the right moves at the right time.

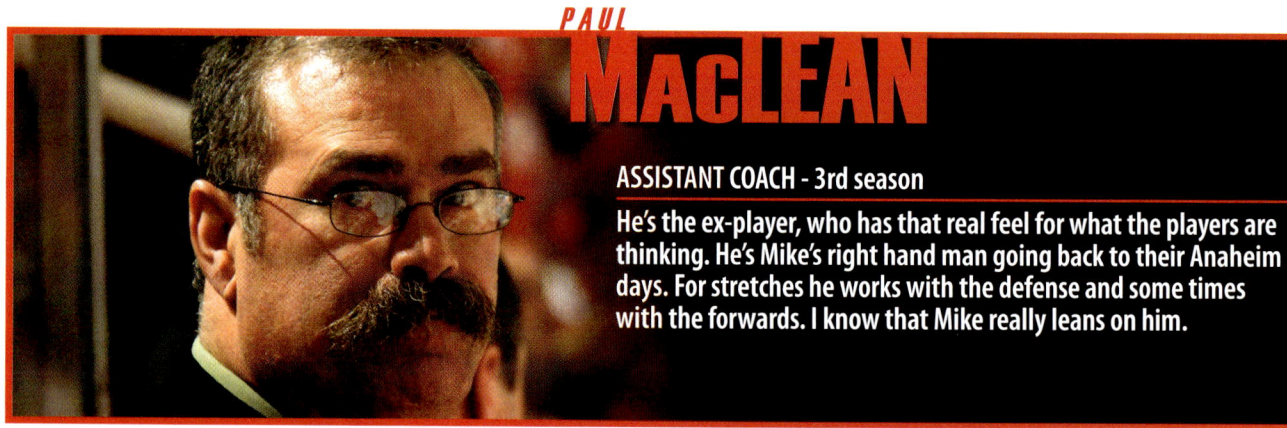

PAUL MacLEAN

ASSISTANT COACH - 3rd season

He's the ex-player, who has that real feel for what the players are thinking. He's Mike's right hand man going back to their Anaheim days. For stretches he works with the defense and some times with the forwards. I know that Mike really leans on him.

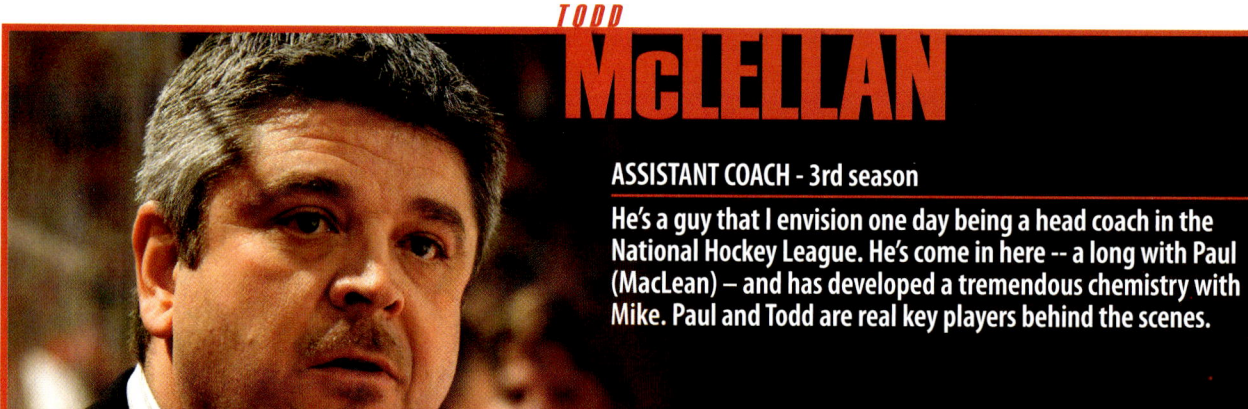

TODD McLELLAN

ASSISTANT COACH - 3rd season

He's a guy that I envision one day being a head coach in the National Hockey League. He's come in here -- a long with Paul (MacLean) – and has developed a tremendous chemistry with Mike. Paul and Todd are real key players behind the scenes.

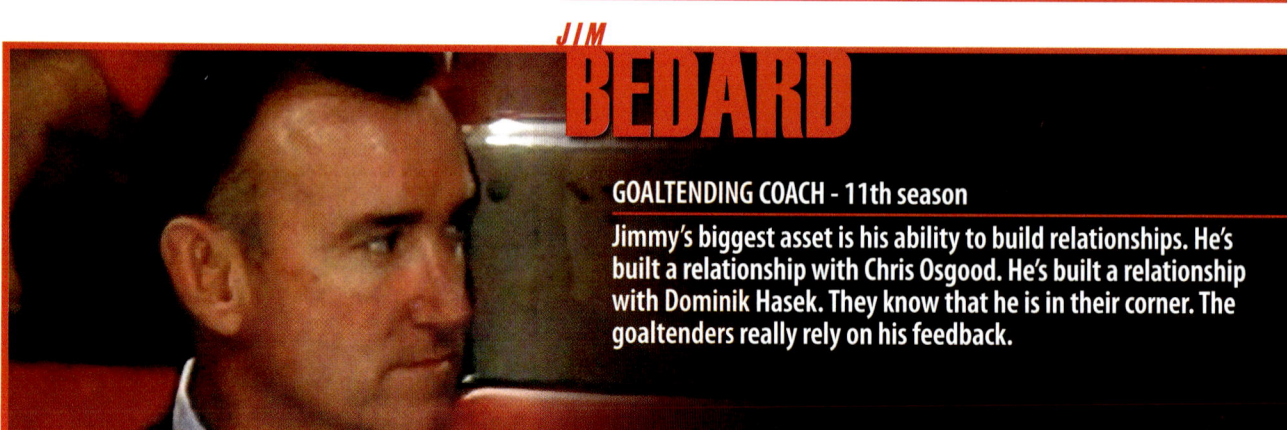

JIM BEDARD

GOALTENDING COACH - 11th season

Jimmy's biggest asset is his ability to build relationships. He's built a relationship with Chris Osgood. He's built a relationship with Dominik Hasek. They know that he is in their corner. The goaltenders really rely on his feedback.

2007-08 STANLEY CUP CHAMPIONS

CAN YOU AFFORD NOT TO BE IN GOOD HANDS®?

ONLY YOUR CHOICE AUTO™ HAS ALL THESE WAYS YOU CAN SAVE STARTING THE DAY YOU SIGN UP.

 **GET A CHECK** every 6 months you don't have an accident. Only Allstate will send you a *Safe Driving Bonus℠ Check* for up to 5% back. It's a bonus on top of any discounts you already receive.

— AND —

 **NO RATE INCREASE** just because of an accident. Other companies make you wait years to get this added protection against rates that could shoot up as much as 40%. Only Allstate offers *Accident Forgiveness* right away.

— AND —

 **$100 OFF** your deductible **IMMEDIATELY.** And that's just for starters. With *Deductible Rewards*,℠ you get an additional $100 off for every year you don't have an accident. Up to $500.

— AND —

 **GET A TOTALLY NEW CAR** if you total your new car during the first three model years. With *New Car Replacement*, you can get a totally new car. Not just the depreciated value, which could be thousands less than you paid.

 **CALL AN ALLSTATE AGENT OR 1-888-ALLSTATE**

2007-2008 THE SEASON

DECEMBER 15, 2007

Babcock gets career win No. 200

By Bill Roose

History was made tonight at Joe Louis Arena.

A Red Wings' victory over the visiting Florida Panthers solidified Mike Babcock in the pages of the franchise's record book.

With a 5-2 win, Babcock reached career-coaching win No. 200, which makes him the second fastest coach to reach the milestone in club history.

Former Wings coach Tommy Ivan needed 353 games to reach 200 wins. Babcock has coached 358 games in less than 4 ½ NHL seasons.

"The first thing I want to do is win, let's get that straight," Babcock said. "It means that you've lasted in the league a little bit, and you've been real fortunate to coach really good players."

Last season, Babcock became the second-fastest NHL coach to win 100 games with a team. He also became the first Wings' coach to lead the club to back-to-back 50-win seasons, something the club eventually did again this season.

"We've been on a good run here since I've been in Detroit and we've won a lot of games with a lot of high-end players who play real hard and play real well," Babcock said. "It's great to be part of a franchise that's doing good things on a consistent basis. And obviously, when the team does well there's lots of individual successes a long the way."

The feeling about Babcock has been mutual for the players in the locker room.

"It helped when he took over right after the lockout," captain Nicklas Lidstrom said. "We still had some of the faces that have been here for a while, but we needed someone new, someone fresh. So he was a good fit for the team when he came here."

Prior to picking Babcock for the coaching gig in Hockeytown, general manager Ken Holland sought a tougher game manager.

"Coming out of the work-stoppage when we made the decision that we were going to go in a different direction behind the bench," Holland said, "I was looking for somebody who was going to be a little bit more demanding. The things I knew about Mike before coming here is that he had tremendous passion. He loves hockey and he has a real good work ethic. I know he's demanding. He's strong in his beliefs and nobody's going to come in and push him over."

Babcock has had the Midas touch wherever he's been. He led the senior Canadian team to the World Championship in 2004, and he's the only Canadian coach to lead both the senior and junior teams to World Championship tourneys.

Prior to accepting the Wings' post, Babcock coached Anaheim to its first Stanley Cup finals appearance in 2003.

"He brings intensity and he really pays attention to details whether it's our systems or if we're getting too sloppy out there," Lidstrom said. "It's not different than other coaches, but he really pays attention to the little details all of the time."

Under Babcock, no stone is left unturned, which is why the NHL-leading Red Wings haven't endured a four-game stretch without getting a single point in two-plus seasons.

It's been a perfect storm.

"What we were getting was younger, quicker and harder, so it kind of arrived at the same time," Babcock said. "I think timing is everything in coaching, and I think it's the same way in playing; you have to arrive at the right time. If you're a shortstop and you arrive in Baltimore when Cal Ripken is in his second year, you're probably not going to get to play. The same thing with coaching, you have to arrive at the right time. The talent has to be there and I've been fortunate."

Currently, the team is on a seven game winning streak. They lead the league with 46 points – 12 points ahead of St. Louis and Columbus in the Central Division.

The Wings' power play and penalty-kill units have been among the league-best under Babcock and his assistants Paul MacLean and Todd McLellan.

This season, the Wings' power play is fourth best, scoring 33 goals on 149 chances. The penalty-kill is equally stellar, holding opponents to 20 goals on 150 man-advantages.

Babcock's philosophy coupled with the abundance of talent at his disposal has created a perfect storm.

"He made some changes and he put his touch on the way we play and it's been working good," said Henrik Zetterberg, the Wings' leading scorer. "The team that we've had here since he's been coaching is pretty good, too.

"It's a real good mix, the pace of the game. We skate a lot and we work a lot. We try to do everything at a high pace, and we've got the skill in this room to do that, and he brings the fastest game out of us. It's a fun way to play."

For Babcock, he says coaching success is all about being consistent.

"If you never had to make hard decisions, or keep people accountable, anybody could be the coach," Babcock said. "I've learned a lot from Scotty (Bowman). It's not about being their friend. It's not about being social with them. It's about getting them to play at the top of their game as much as you possibly can . . . without grinding on them. That's the fine line. How do you do it over 82 games, every year without grinding them to death?"

Is Babcock's methodology always viewed positively in the locker room?

"Not always," Zetterbreg said. "His way of playing is a little different. But we always have a discussion if there's something that we don't like and want to change a bit. I think that's real important to have. . . . He has an open approach."

Detroit Red Wings
SEASON HIGHLIGHTS

Right: Babcock shared a light moment with the media following the Wings' 4-2 win over Nashville in Game 2 of the Western Conference quarterfinal at Joe Louis Arena.

Below: A shift in momentum during Game 2 against Nashville occurred when Babcock used his timeout moments after Nashville tied the score in the second period. Seconds later, the Wings regained the lead on a Kris Draper score. (Photo by Gregory Shamus/Getty Images)

Bottom: Coaching in the All-Star Game was a thrill for Babcock, who shared an idea with Western Conference All-Star Chris Pronger during practice at Atlanta's Philips Arena in January. (Photo by Dave Sandford/Getty Images)

2007-08 STANLEY CUP CHAMPIONS

DETROIT RED WINGS SEASON HIGHLIGHTS

JANUARY 8, 2008

Chelios becomes second-oldest player

By Bill Roose

Bellow: Chris Chelios waves to fans after being announced as the second oldest player to play in a NHL game on January 8. (Photo by Gregory Shamus/Getty Images)

Bottom Left: One of the things that Chelios still does well is battle in front of the net, as he did here against Nashville's Radek Bonk during Game 3 of the Western Conference quarterfinal at the Sommet Center. (Photo by John Russell/NHLI via Getty Images)

Top Left: Chelios entered the league with the Montreal Canadians. (Photo by Montreal Canadians hockey club)

It was nearly this time last season that Red Wings defenseman Chris Chelios first learned of Moe Roberts, a retired journeyman goalie, who suited up for the Chicago Blackhawks for one last time more than 56 years ago.

Roberts was an assistant trainer for the Blackhawks when goalie Harry Lumley was injured in a game against the Red Wings. Just 19 days shy of his 46th birthday, Roberts donned the goalie gear and finished the game.

Tonight, Chelios will pass Roberts as the second-oldest player in NHL history at 45 years and 348 days when the Wings host the Colorado Avalanche at Joe Louis Arena.

Entering Tuesday's game, Chelios has logged 1,586 games in 23 ½ NHL seasons.

Chelios, who turns 46 on Jan. 25, naturally doesn't feel as good as he did when he entered the league as a rookie with Montreal in 1983-84, but he doesn't plan to set a timetable for retirement, either.

"Do I feel as good? No," said Chelios with a good laugh. "But I feel good enough. I haven't had anything significant or chronic, so I feel good. … As good as I'm gonna feel."

Wings legend Gordie Howe holds the distinction of being the oldest player in league history, having played his final game on April 6, 1980. Howe was 52 years and six days.

For Chelios to pass Howe, means the three-time Norris Trophy winner would have to still be playing on Feb. 1, 2014.

"We'll see," said Chelios, who is older than seven current NHL coaches. "I don't want to say something then jinks myself. For the time being, just don't think about it and keep going. As long as we're winning, it gives me a chance to keep playing."

Asked about his longevity, he added, "It's lucky and being very fortunate, and being in the right place at the right time. I don't think I'm going to attributive it to the sauna. That helps me from not getting colds and the flu. It's just lucky."

2007-08 STANLEY CUP CHAMPIONS

Congratulations on number 11!

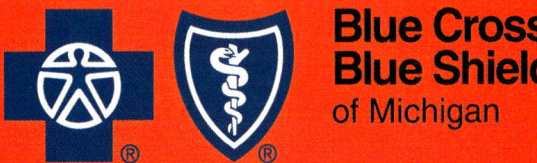

bcbsm.com

DETROIT RED WINGS
SEASON HIGHLIGHTS

MARCH 28, 2008

Drake reminded of his longevity: Wings' forward reaches 1,000

By Kevin Fitzhenry

The 1,000-game milestone has perhaps lost some of its luster over the years with 30 franchise clubs and over 700 players currently in the NHL. Not since the days of the Original Six has playing 1,000 games been considered a major accomplishment.

But that won't tarnish the achievement for one Red Wings' player.

"It just means you've been in the league a long time," said right wing Dallas Drake, who played in his 1,000th career game when the Red Wings hosted the Chicago Blackhawks on March 11.

"Not a lot of guys get the opportunity to play as long as I have," Drake said. "Early on in your career you're just trying to stay in the league as long as you can. Then, big picture is you want to win the Stanley Cup."

Only two other current Red Wings -- defensemen Nicklas Lidstrom (1,239) and Chris Chelios (1,605) -- have played more games. Left wing Kirk Maltby (931) and center Kris Draper (945) could possibly reach the milestone as early as next season.

Drake, who was drafted by the Red Wings in the sixth round of the 1989 draft, played only 119 games in Detroit before being traded to the Winnipeg Jets. He played in St. Louis for six seasons before signing with Detroit as a free agent last July.

"It's a huge accomplishment," Wings coach Mike Babcock said. "He's a great addition to our hockey club because of the integrity, commitment, character, and how hard he plays the game. When you bring in good people it's contagious. He has lot a fun with the game; he's here first thing in the morning and he wants to play. It's a real honor to have him here."

During the March 11 game, many of Drake's former teammates congratulated him via taped messages on the JLA Jumbotron over center ice.

Drake said he certainly appreciates the thoughts of his teammates.

"You ask any player and that's what they miss the most about the game … is the camaraderie of the dressing room," he said. "No matter what happens, you can always have a good time with the guys."

Drake helped the Wings to an early 1-0 lead when he assisted on Maltby's first-period goal. It was career assist No. 300 for Drake -- yet another milestone.

Left: On March 28, Drake was congratulated by the captains – Wings' Nicklas Lidstrom and St. Louis' Keith Tkachuk -- during a pre-game ceremony to recognize Drake's 1,000th NHL game, which was March 11.

Above: Drake celebrated his tying goal against Buffalo and goalie Ryan Miller at HSBC Arena in March. It was Drake's final goal of the regular-season in career game No. 997. (Photo by Bill Wippert/NHLI via Getty Images)

2007-08 STANLEY CUP CHAMPIONS

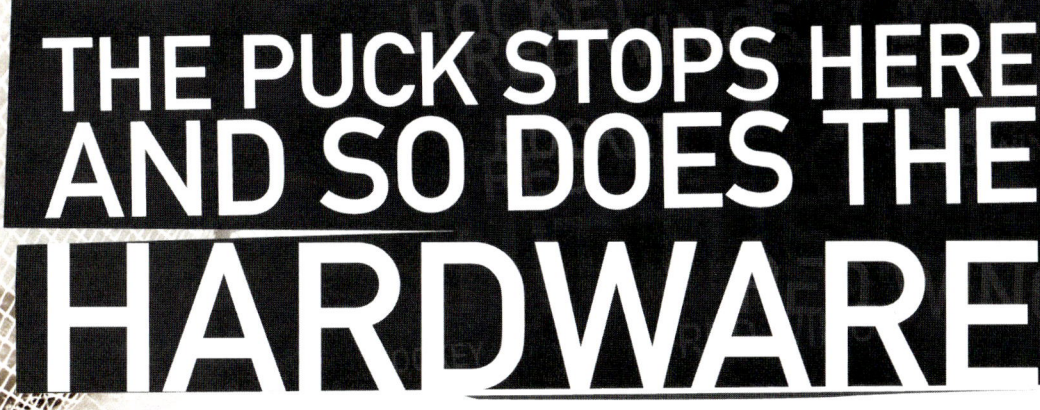

THE PUCK STOPS HERE AND SO DOES THE HARDWARE

HOCKEYTOWN WINS IT ALL.

CONGRATULATIONS RED WINGS, FROM OUR #1 TEAM TO YOURS.

© 2008 The Kroger Co.

DETROIT RED WINGS
SEASON HIGHLIGHTS

MAY 24, 2008

Even in the new cap era, Holland proves his excellence

By Lindsey Ungar

There's been so-called dynasties in the modern NHL before. The Montreal Canadiens won four straight Stanley Cups from 1976-79. The New York Islanders and Edmonton Oilers took their turns wreaking havoc on the league in the 1980s.

But with further expansion, free agency and now, a salary cap, that was supposed to come to an end. And parity was to begin.

The Red Wings apparently missed that league memo.

Beginning Saturday night, the Wings enter the Stanley Cup finals looking for their fourth championship in 11 years. They've barely flinched since 1990-91 — the last time they had a losing season.

"The team doesn't seem to slow down," forward Dallas Drake said of the run.

Especially not since Ken Holland took over as general manager in July 1997. Since then, the Red Wings have won eight Central Division titles, eight regular-season Western Conference titles, two Stanley Cups and four Presidents' trophies.

That's a lot accomplished in 11 years. But Holland has been behind the scenes at the Red Wings since 1985, when he started as a scout in western Canada. The current front office, including assistant manager Jim Nill, director of amateur scouting Joe McDonnell and director of European scouting Hakan Andersson, started assembling soon after.

"By the mid-90s, our entire scouting team was together," Holland said. "I think there's real good chemistry between our scouts because of how long they've worked together."

That cohesiveness and a yearly commitment to a puck-possession philosophy are just part of the equation. Having Nicklas Lidstrom — who Holland called "the best defenseman in the world for a decade" — hasn't hurt, either.

But it can't all be hockey smarts and Lidstrom, right?

"It's funny how it works sometimes you gotta be lucky," Holland said.

Lucky they were when it came to finding one of their current superstars, leading playoff scorer Henrik Zetterberg.

Nill and Andersson were on a scouting mission in northern Sweden to watch Mattias Weinhandl. Instead, they happened to notice this "little guy," Holland said.

That little guy was Zetterberg. On the scouts' recommendation, the Red Wings selected Zetterberg in the seventh round — 210th overall — in the 1999 draft.

"And the rest is history," Holland said.

Through the Western Conference finals, Zetterberg led the playoffs in scoring and was four wins away from his first Stanley Cup. Weinhandl, who ended up as a third-rounder in 1999, played just 182 NHL games before returning to the Swedish Elite League this season.

That isn't the only gem this scouting staff has discovered: Pavel Datsyuk (sixth), Johan Franzen (third) and Valtteri Filppula (third) were all later picks.

Pittsburgh general manager Ray Shero called Detroit the "model franchise." But not just because of drafting — free agent signings and deadline deals, as well.

Last summer, Holland brought in Brian Rafalski to replace Mathieu Schneider on the blue line. At the deadline, Holland traded a couple of draft picks for Brad Stuart. Both defensemen now play in Detroit's top four.

Shero has been personally victimized by the Red Wings success in the past — he spent eight years as the assistant GM in Nashville before joining the Penguins.

"They'd be at $70 million, we'd be at $20 million at payroll, and we'd always say, 'Wait until they straighten this labor thing out, we're going to get these guys.'

"Well, great job. They've come back and new labor agreement or not, Kenny shows what a great job he does and they're a top team again, and I think that's a testament to the job he does and the staff he has."

The year before the lockout, the Red Wings' payroll was almost $80 million. Now, it's about $30 million less, a result of a capped economy.

But the results for the Wings haven't changed — at least in the regular-season. They still haven't won a Stanley Cup in the new era, but that could change soon – real soon. And if it doesn't, Holland and company will stick to the plan that has kept them successful for more than a decade.

"It's about living in the present and doing it your way," Wings coach Mike Babcock said. "And having a philosophy, and doing it right and sticking to your plan. I think that's what happens here. Sometimes, for example, three years ago, we had 124 points, fifth-best of all time and we lost in the first round. It's so easy to blow up your team and say there's a lot wrong with it, while there's obviously a lot right with it. Just make it better and keep adjusting."

2007-08 STANLEY CUP CHAMPIONS

DETROIT RED WINGS
SEASON HIGHLIGHTS

MAY 24, 2008

Birthday Bandit leads locker room goofiness

By Michael Caples

Kris Draper is known for many things. He's a face off wizard, a shutdown defensive forward, and one of the quickest skaters in the NHL. But in the Red Wings' locker room, he plays an even more important role – birthday prankster.

Draper, who has been dubbed the "Birthday Bandit" by his teammates, leads the Wings in the goofing-around department. The 37-year-old center, who has spent 12 seasons in Detroit, says that pranks and jokes are important to keeping the game enjoyable over a 10-month grueling season.

"You're going to have those days where it's like a here-we-go-again kind of thing, and it's something that's been fun," Draper said. "I think a lot of guys got involved with it, helping out, getting guys. There's some good stuff with it."

The Bandit said he has always tried to inspire his teammates before and during games, but he's quick to point out how many great leaders the Wings have been fortunate to have.

"I think I've always tried to be vocal in this locker room," he said. "We've always had great leaders in this room that had a great feel for when to say things. I kind of looked at just being a little bit more of a rah-rah guy in between, on the bench and in between periods. It's always something that I've tried to do."

Draper's main prank is the birthday shaving cream pie, where he loads up a towel with gel foam and catches his teammate when he least expects it.

This year's targets have included Jiri Hudler, Henrik Zetterberg, Chris Osgood and Dan Cleary. Draper also received help from his friend Kirk Maltby, who managed to pie tough guy Darren McCarty.

However, there's a unwritten rule that veteran players, like Chris Chelios and Nicklas Lidstrom, are off limits.

"Cheli threatened to slash my tires if I went after him," said Draper, laughing. "Nick, ya know, perfect human and it's just Nick. I told him, 'just so you know, it won't be me getting you.'"

Hudler said that he's never been part of a locker room that has this much fun.

"It's unbelievable," he said. "If I try to go home after the season, try to explain to my friends, my ex-teammates, they probably won't believe me in how this locker room is fun with all the stars, legends and future hall-of-famers."

Only in Hockeytown.

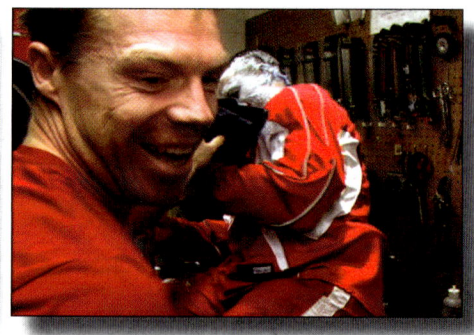

2007-08 STANLEY CUP CHAMPIONS

DETROIT RED WINGS
SEASON HIGHLIGHTS

MAY 5, 2008

Longevity Lidstrom: Captain's stamina, ability drives Wings' championship run

By Bill Roose

When general manager Ken Holland afforded captain Nicklas Lidstrom a new two-year contract in December, the deal came with some pretty flattering praise for the five-time Norris Trophy winner.

"Nick has been the best defenseman in the world for several years," Holland said. "He's a great captain and role model who does everything right both on and off the ice. We're proud to have him continue as a Red Wing for another two years."

Since joining the Red Wings as a third round draft pick in 1989, Lidstrom has been more than a model citizen, exceeding all expectations of a gratified front office staff, while drawing comparisons to such notable greats as Bobby Orr and Doug Harvey. He's often regarded as the best European ever to play in the NHL, and other than Orr (eight) and Harvey (seven) nobody has collected more Norris trophies as the league's top defenseman.

Lidstrom isn't flashy on the ice or otherwise, but when it comes to igniting the Wings' lethal offense, nobody does it better than Lidstrom, who led all defensemen in scoring this season with 10 goals and 60 assists.

He turned 38 in April, but Holland doesn't believe this will be Lidstrom's final contract with the Wings.

"Certainly the superstars, it appears to me, can play into their early 40s," Holland said. "We've had guys like Steve Yzerman who was a real good player for us in his late 30s. Chris Chelios at the age of 46 is still going strong.

"I think there's no reason to think that Nick can't continue to play at the level he's at for the next two or three years. Again, if he continues to stay healthy, Nick plays such a smart game, it's all about positioning, the ability to move the puck."

Luckily for the Wings, the one time in his career that Lidstrom found himself in a vulnerable spot, he only missed six games with a sprained knee after Colorado forward Ian Laperriere checked him into the boards in Denver.

"Again, for the next two or three years I don't see any reason why he can't continue to play at the level he's at," Holland said. "Beyond that I think, again, it depends on health, and I also think it probably depends on passion.

"As long as Nick loves going to the rink, loves to play hockey, healthy, I think he can remain one of the top defensemen here for a few years."

Lidstrom's statistics speak volumes for what he has meant to the Red Wings for the past 16 seasons.

Four Stanley Cup titles and he'll likely win a sixth Norris in June -- after earning a ninth nomination in the last 10 seasons – for helping the Wings post the NHL's best defensive record in 2007-08. He ranked second in the league to Pavel Datsyuk in plus-minus (plus-40) and was fourth among all players in average ice time per game (26:43).

The longevity stat is amazing. In Game 5 of the Western Conference quarterfinal against Nashville, Lidstrom passed Yzerman for most playoff games in franchise history with 197.

As a comparison to the two defensemen that Lidstrom's most compared, Harvey played 1,113 regular-season games and 137 playoff contests in 20 seasons. Knee injuries obviously cost Orr, who played in a total of 731 NHL games.

Lidstrom has played in as many regular-season games (1,250) as Harvey did in regular-season and playoffs combined in four fewer years than Lidstrom. As for Orr, he played in 41.5 percent fewer games than Lidstrom.

"We know that every time that Nick comes to the rink he's going to be one of our best players, if not the best player, night in and night out," Kris Draper said. "The playoff (record) is unbelievable and that's something that you probably ask anybody, that's something that you're going to be most proud of, most games played at this time of year. It shows that he's been on great regular-season teams and he's had some great playoff runs. That's something that he should certainly be proud of."

LITTLE FOXES FINE GIFTS

Unique Gifts from Around the World

MacKenzie-Childs

Baccarat

Spode

WILLIAM YEOWARD

Herend

WATERFORD

Moser

Vera Bradley

and Many More!

Visit our store located in the Historic Fox Theatre Building in Downtown Detroit, online at LittleFoxes.com or call 313.983.6202 today!

LittleFoxes.com

DETROIT RED WINGS
SEASON HIGHLIGHTS

DECEMBER 17, 2007

Penalty shots put Filppula in exclusive company

By Bill Roose

In only his second full season in the NHL and Valtteri Filppula is already rubbing elbows with some pretty impressive company in the Red Wings' record book.

On Saturday, Filppula scored his second penalty shot goal in less than a week, becoming only the fourth player to score multiple career penalty shot goals in franchise history.

The exclusive group that Filppula has been granted membership consists of hockey hall of famers Gordie Howe and Ebbie Goodfellow, and longtime captain and certain future hall-of-famer Steve Yzerman.

"Obviously, they are very big names, and they were great players," Filppula said. "I don't think I'm there, not even close. But it's weird for me to have two penalty shots already at this time of the season. ... It doesn't happen too often."

Filppula beat Florida goalie Tomas Vokoun in the third period last Saturday. The Wings center waited for Vokoun to commit before going to his backhand and lifting a shot over the Panthers' goalie. The same move was successful for Filppula against Nashville goalie Dan Ellis last Monday.

"The first one in Nashville, I really want to shoot, I was thinking about shooting," Filppula said, "but then the goalie was so far away from the net, so I changed my mind about halfway.

"Last game I wanted to go the same way because it worked earlier. It was a pretty simple move."

Dan Cleary scored a penalty shot goal for the Wings last season, beating Calgary goalie Miikka Kiprusoff in Game 5 of the Western Conference quarterfinal. It was just the second successful penalty shot in Wings' playoff history.

But Filppula's goal in Nashville broke a Wings' string of nine unsuccessful, regular-season penalty shots. The previous successful penalty shot for the Wings occurred when Igor Larionov beat San Jose's Arturs Irbe on Nov. 22, 1995.

Filppula's teammates have been impressed with his composure.

"He's got a lot of skill when it comes down to penalty shots," Henrik Zetterberg said. "The last two moves have been real nice, and he looks real calm and not nervous at all when he steps up to the puck."

Asked if opposing goalies will begin reading the scouting reports on Filppula's backhand move, Zetterberg said, "It's tough for the goalie to read though. He has another move where he goes to the forward too, so that's not his only move, and if the goalie is going to read him he's just going to do something else." **DR**

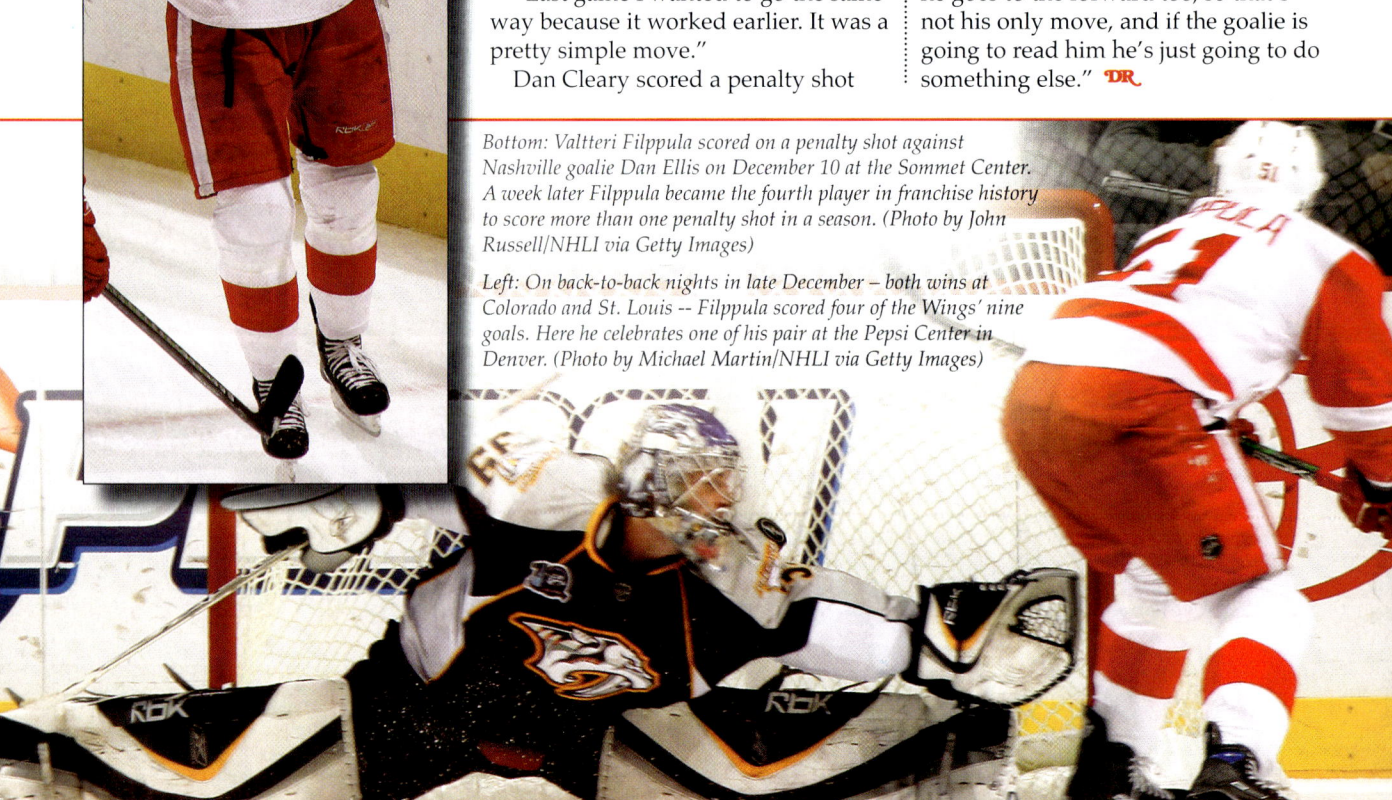

Bottom: Valtteri Filppula scored on a penalty shot against Nashville goalie Dan Ellis on December 10 at the Sommet Center. A week later Filppula became the fourth player in franchise history to score more than one penalty shot in a season. (Photo by John Russell/NHLI via Getty Images)

Left: On back-to-back nights in late December – both wins at Colorado and St. Louis -- Filppula scored four of the Wings' nine goals. Here he celebrates one of his pair at the Pepsi Center in Denver. (Photo by Michael Martin/NHLI via Getty Images)

2007-08 STANLEY CUP CHAMPIONS

To the Red Wings from the Red Tails: Congratulations!

From our team to yours, congratulations on an outstanding season.

FEBRUARY 25, 2008

McCarty returns home, signs with Red Wings

By Bill Roose

Darren McCarty drove from Grand Rapids in the early morning hours Monday to accept the Red Wings' one-year contract offer to rejoin a franchise that he once played for in 11 NHL seasons.

After signing the contract, McCarty visited with old friends and ran into captain Nicklas Lidstrom in the Red Wings' locker room at Joe Louis Arena.

"It's nice to come back and see some familiar faces," McCarty said. "It's just the beginning and I plan, when I get up, to help this team win."

McCarty will return to Grand Rapids and continue a two-week conditioning assignment. From there he'll likely rejoin the Red Wings with the hopes of winning a roster spot, Wings general manager Ken Holland said.

"At some point in time he will be with the Red Wings," Holland said. "Now it's up to the coaching staff to determine if he can help us. And it's up to Darren McCarty.

"He has six weeks before the playoffs start to win Mike Babcock and his coaches over. The worse case scenario is that he doesn't get in there regularly, but he continues to improve. He's good insurance. He's been in the playoffs before. He knows what the playoffs are all about. He has a physical presence. Our hope is that he can do more than that."

McCarty, 35, could be in a Red Wings' uniform as early as mid-March when Detroit hosts Chicago, Dallas and Nashville in a five-day stretch.

McCarty has been working the last several months to get back to the NHL. He confided in his friends, most notably Chris Osgood and Kris Draper, who helped get McCarty back into a workout routine and signed with the Flint Generals in the International Hockey League.

After an 11 game stint with the Generals, the Wings signed McCarty to a pro tryout contract on Feb. 1. In nine games with the Griffins, he has four goals and three assists.

The Griffins played in Quad City on Sunday, and returned to Grand Rapids about 3 a.m. Monday. From there, McCarty traveled to Detroit to sign the deal.

He admits that in the past he never thought this day would ever come. But more recently he's allowed himself to believe that it could.

"I always hoped," McCarty said. "One of the biggest disappointments was having to leave. But it's funny how life works itself out and I can really relate to talking to Ozzie about leaving and coming back.

To the delight of the Joe Louis Arena crowd, McCarty is congratulated by teammates after his first period goal against the Predators in Game 2 of the Western Conference quarterfinal. (Photo by Gregory Shamus/Getty Images)

"I had to change some things in my life. I had to change, and I think that where I'm at now is what has made me successful here and has made me an integral part in winning some championships. That's sort of the character and things that I'm prepared to bring in the dressing room and on the ice. I can't express my excitement."

McCarty was a fixture for the Wings from 1993 until the lockout season in 2004. The next year he signed with Calgary, where he remained for two seasons, compiling seven goals and 13 assists in 99 games with the Flames. McCarty was a member of three Stanley Cup winning teams, and forged a memorable trio known as the Grind Line with Kirk Maltby and Draper during his first stint in Hockeytown.

"After the work-stoppage, I thought he lost his focus and his passion for the game," Holland said. "I think that over the last 6-10 months he has got his life in order and we're going to give him an opportunity to show us what he can do."

According to the CBA, the Red Wings had until Tuesday's 3 p.m. ET trade deadline to reach a deal with McCarty. But Holland said that the team had come to the conclusion over the weekend to sign the veteran forward.

"Ultimately, I would say to you we made this move based on his history with us," Holland said. "I think he has his focus and passion back for hockey, he's got his priorities of sobriety in order, his family and hockey. Again, we're going to take a flyer on him. There's no guarantee that he's going to come in and be the answer. But let's see."

DETROIT RED WINGS
SEASON HIGHLIGHTS

Right: Always a fan favorite, a small fan showed his affection for D Mac's return on March 28. "The response from the people, it almost becomes uncomfortable, but in a good way," McCarty said. "I really appreciate all of that."

Below: After the Wings throttled the Avalanche early in Game 2 of the Western Conference semifinal, McCarty took care of Colorado tough guy Cody McCormick. (Photo by Gregory Shamus/Getty Images)

2007-08 STANLEY CUP CHAMPIONS

SEASON HIGHLIGHTS

NOVEMBER 13, 2007

Red Bird stuck, team spends night in St. Louis

By Bill Roose

The one thing the Red Wings didn't want to do after a 4-3 loss to the Blues was to spend an extra night in the Gateway City.

But that's exactly what they were forced to do after their plane became stuck in the mud at St. Louis Downtown Airport in Cahokia.

Team spokesman John Hahn reports that the rear right wheels of Red Bird II inadvertently crossed into the grass next to the tarmac. Due to heavy rains in the St. Louis area the prior day, the wheels sank into the mud and the plane was not able to dislodge under its own power.

The plane was traveling at approximately five miles per hour at the time.

The Red Wings disembarked in a normal manner and returned to their team hotel in St. Louis for the evening. They eventually returned to Detroit a day later via a charter flight.

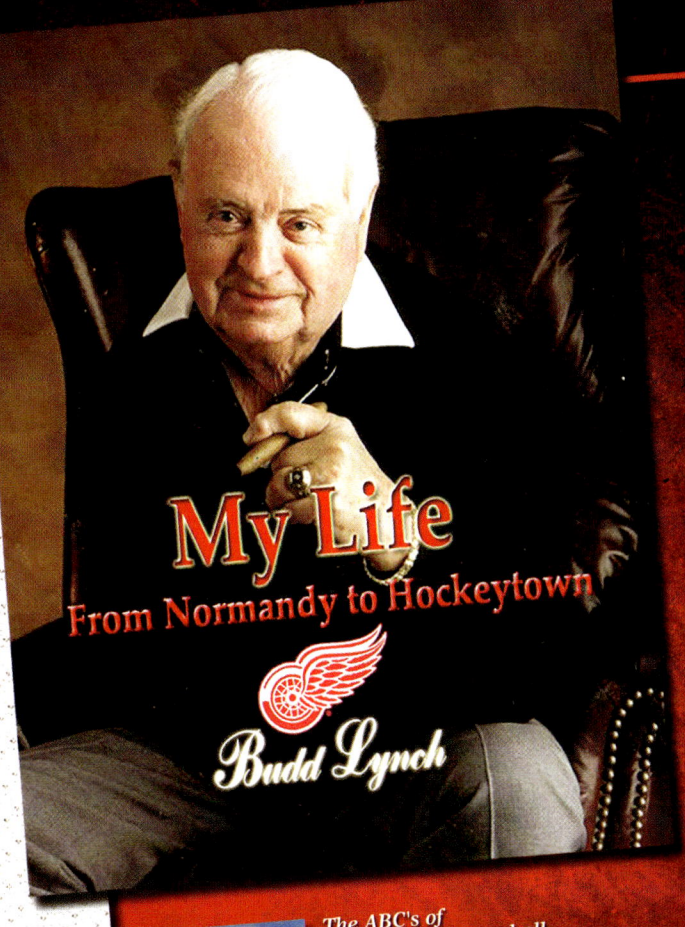

DETROIT RED WINGS
SEASON HIGHLIGHTS

FEBRUARY 26, 2008

Wings add depth on blueline, deal for LA's Stuart

By Bill Roose

At Tuesday's 3 p.m. trade deadline, the Red Wings added depth to their blue line, acquiring veteran defenseman Brad Stuart from the Los Angeles Kings.

"Last year in the Calgary series, we thought he was one of their better defensemen against us in the first round," general manager Ken Holland said. "He plays abrasive. At playoff time he gives us depth on defense."

In last spring's playoff series against Calgary – won by the Red Wings in six games – Stuart played in all six games with the Flames, tallying one assist.

"He can play on the second power play, he can kill penalties," Holland said. "You can never have enough defensemen as we saw last year in our playoff run."

In return for the eight-year veteran, the Kings receive the Red Wings' second round draft pick in 2008, and fourth round selection in 2009.

"He's gritty and has some size and he'll give us a different dimension," Holland said.

Stuart's acquisition comes at a time when the Red Wings need some help on the blue line with four defensemen currently on the injury list -- captain Nicklas Lidstrom (knee), Brian Rafalski (groin), Niklas Kronwall (clavicle) and Chris Chelios (leg).

In 63 games with the Kings, Stuart, from Rocky Mountain House, Alberta, had five goals and 16 assists. In his last game against the Red Wings, Stuart tied a career-high by collecting three points in LA's 5-3 comeback victory on Feb. 7 at Joe Louis Arena.

Last summer, Stuart signed a one-year deal with Los Angeles. But before doing so, his agent had some conversations with Holland about potentially coming to Detroit.

"I talked to his agent a lot this summer when he was a free agent," Holland said. "In the end, he's married to a girl from California and he ended up signing a one-year deal with LA. So he's been someone that we've liked."

Detroit is Stuart's fifth NHL franchise. The first-round pick (third overall) of the San Jose Sharks in 1998, Stuart has also played for Boston.

His best statistical season occurred in 2005-06, while splitting time between San Jose and Boston. That season, Stuart had 12 goals and 31 assists.

Stuart, 28, was part of the blockbuster deal that sent Joe Thornton to San Jose in Nov. 2005.

"He's going to play physical," Holland said. "He's got good size to him. He's going to move the puck up. We have seven established defensemen and we add a veteran defenseman.

"We feel good about (Derek) Meech, and (Kyle) Quincey and (Jonathan) Ericsson. But playoffs are still about winning 2-1, 3-2 and 1-0 as we saw last year in the playoffs. We're not looking at (Stuart) to get points. We see him chipping in with a little offense. He's gritty and has some size and he'll give us a different dimension."

Below: Brad Stuart has chipped in with a physical brand of defense, like drilling Stars' Joel Lundqvist into the boards during Game 2 of the Western Conference finals at Joe Louis Arena. (Photo by Dave Sandford/Getty Images)

Above: A broken finger limited Stuart's action as a Red Wing to nine regular-season games. But in the playoffs, he didn't miss a beat partnered with Niklas Kronwall.

2007-08 STANLEY CUP CHAMPIONS

Get an assist with every purchase.

se the new Detroit Red Wings Platinum Plus® MasterCard® credit ard with WorldPoints® rewards everywhere you shop and earn nlimited cash rewards, travel on major U.S. airlines with no ackout dates, brand-name merchandise, and gift cards to top etailers. You'll even receive a Detroit Red Wings woven blanket fter your first qualifying transaction(s).◆

FREE◆
Detroit Red Wings woven blanket
after qualifying transaction(s)

Call 1.800.438.6262
nd mention priority code FABTQ5.

◆ To receive the Detroit Red Wings woven blanket, apply for the card, then upon approval, use it to make any combination of purchases, balance transfers, or cash advance ansactions totaling at least $75 (excludes transaction fees, if any): all qualifying transactions must occur within the same billing cycle ending on or before August 30, 2008. Limit e (est. retail value of $50) per new account. Please allow 8-12 weeks for delivery after qualifying transactions. Supplies are limited. Offer sponsored by FIA Card Services, N.A.; we ay substitute an item of equal or greater value and are not responsible for lost or stolen merchandise.

ere are costs associated with the use of this credit card. To request specific information about the costs, you may contact FIA Card Services, N.A., by calling 800.438.6262 or writing to P.O. Box 15020, Wilmington, DE 19850. TTY users, call 1.800.833.6262. This credit card program is issued and administered by FIA Card ervices, N.A. The WorldPoints program is managed in part by independent third parties, including a travel agency registered to do business in California (Reg. No. 2036509-); Ohio (Reg. No. 87890286); Washington (6011237430) and other states, as required. For more information about the program, visit www.bankofamerica.com/worldpoints. asterCard is a registered trademark of MasterCard International Incorporated, and is used by the issuer pursuant to license. WorldPoints and Platinum Plus are registered ademarks of FIA Card Services, N.A. Bank of America and the Bank of America logo are registered trademarks of Bank of America Corporation. NHL is a registered trademark d the NHL Shield is a trademark of the National Hockey League. All NHL logos and marks and team logos and marks depicted herein are the property of the NHL and the spective teams and may not be reproduced without the prior written consent of NHL Enterprise, L.P. ©NHL 2007. All rights reserved..

2007 Bank of America Corporation T-708049-080307 BAD-09-07-10425

2007-2008
THE PAST

DETROIT RED WINGS

1935-36 STANLEY CUP CHAMPIONS

Detroit Dominance

Under the coaching guidance of Jack Adams, the Red Wings captured their first Stanley Cup championship after 10 NHL seasons.

Detroit's first bid for Lord Stanley's mug ended in a disappointing four-game loss to Chicago two years prior, but Adams confidently stated that history would not repeat itself. "The Wings are a much stronger team than in 1934," he said.

Blasting their way to the final with a three-game sweep of the Montreal Maroons, only archrival Toronto stood in the way, and Detroit set out to make short work of the Maple Leafs, whipping them 3-1 and 9-4 in the first two games at the Olympia.

The nine goals set a single-game playoff record for the Wings, one that still remains as a franchise-best.

Toronto rallied from a 3-0 deficit with 6:50 to play in regulation time in Game 4, winning 4-3 on Buzz Boll's overtime marker, but the setback was temporary. The Wings overcame a first-period goal by Leafs center Joe Primeau, racing to a 3-1 lead. They held on for a 3-2 win and the first championship in club history.

"Every player on the team has taken a turn at bringing the house down in these playoffs," Adams said. "I never saw anything like it."

The series marked King Clancy's sixth and final appearance as a Maple Leafs' defenseman in the final. However, it would not be his last Stanley Cup series, for Clancy went on to earn prominence as an NHL referee working 20 Stanley Cup games in that capacity. **DR**

Series A Semifinals vs. Montreal Maroons

Date	Visitor	Score	Home	Score
Mar. 24	Detroit	1	Montreal	0 (6OT)
Mar. 26	Detroit	3	Montral	0
Mar. 28	Montreal	1	Detroit	2

Detroit won best-of-five series 3-0

Series E Final vs. Toronto Maple Leafs

Date	Visitor	Score	Home	Score
Apr. 5	Toronto	1	Detroit	3
Apr. 7	Toronto	4	Detroit	9
Apr. 9	Detroit	3	Toronto	4 (OT)
Apr. 11	Detroit	3	Toronto	2

Detroit won best-of-five series 3-1

STANLEY CUP ROSTER
Jack Adams (Coach)

#	NAME	#	NAME
10	John Sorrell	11	Gord Pettinger
8	Syd Howe	3	Bucko McDonald
7	Marty Barry	16	Ralph Bowman
4	Herbie Lewis	15	Pete Kelly
6	Larry Aurie	2	Doug Young C
14	Mud Bruneteau	5	Ebbie Goodfellow
9	Wally Kilrea	1	Normie Smith
12	Hec Kilrea		

2007-08 STANLEY CUP CHAMPIONS

Wings' depth wins Cup

Turned away from Madison Square Garden -- once again by the incoming circus – after Game 1, the New York Rangers agreed to play the rest of the Stanley Cup finals on Detroit's home ice.

Red Wings goalie Earl Robertson became the first rookie to post two shutouts in the finals, blanking the Rangers in the last two games of the series.

With all-stars Larry Aurie and Normie Smith, captain Doug Young and rookie defenseman Orville Roulston all injured, the Wings figured to be in a bind against the Rangers, but Detroit's character carried the day.

Down 2-1 in the series, center Marty Barry stepped forward, scoring the only goal in Detroit's Game 4 win. He also scored a pair, including the Cup-winner, in a 3-0 Game 5 verdict.

"That's one goal for each of the broken-legged guys," Aurie suggested after the clinching win. He was joined on crutches by Young and Roulston, while an elbow injury idled Smith.

"With three all-stars out with injuries, we beat those high-flying Rangers," Wings general manager Jack Adams boasted.

Detroit became the first American team to win successive Stanley Cups by edging the Rangers and joined the Ottawa Senators (1919-20, 1920-21) as the only NHL teams to finish first and win the Cup in back-to-back seasons.

When Smith went down with torn elbow ligaments in the Stanley Cup semifinals, Canadiens general manager Cecil Hart was ready to dance a jig. "I don't see any reason why we shouldn't win it," he said.

Robertson saw things differently.

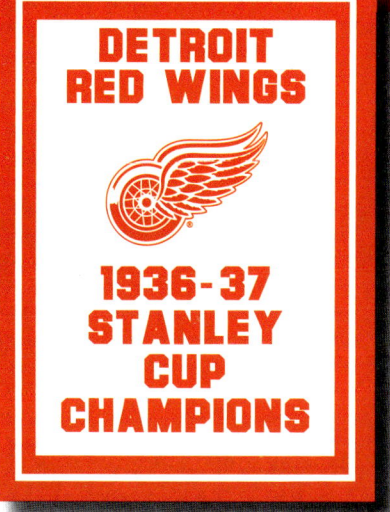

DETROIT RED WINGS

1936-37 STANLEY CUP CHAMPIONS

Called up to make his NHL debut in Game 4 of the best-of-five set against the Habs, Robertson was a 3-1 loser that night, but posted a 2-1 win in Game 5, moving Detroit to the finals against New York.

In another five-game set, Robertson posted shutouts in Games 4 and 5 to clinch the title. "They could take me out and shoot me now," Robertson said. "I'd die happy." **DR**

AURIE

Series A Semifinals vs. Montreal Canadians

Date	Visitor	Score	Home	Score
Mar. 23	Montreal	0	Detroit	4
Mar. 25	Montreal	1	Detroit	5
Mar. 27	Detroit	1	Montreal	3
Mar. 30	Detroit	1	Montreal	3
Apr. 1	Detroit 2	2	Montreal	1 (3OT)

Detroit won best-of-five series 3-2

Series E Final vs. New York Rangers

Date	Visitor	Score	Home	Score
Apr. 6	Detroit	1	NY Rangers	5
Apr. 8	NY Rangers	2	Detroit	4
Apr. 11	NY Rangers	1	Detroit	0
Apr. 13	NY Rangers	0	Detroit	1
Apr. 15	NY Rangers	0	Detroit	3

Detroit won best-of-five series 3-2

STANLEY CUP ROSTER
Jack Adams (Coach)

#	NAME	#	NAME
1	Normie Smith	5	Ebbie Goodfellow
15	Pete Kelly	2	John Gallagher
6	Larry Aurie	16	Ralph Bowman
4	Herbie Lewis	10	John Sorrell
12	Hec Kilrea	7	Marty Barry
14	Mud Bruneteau	1	Earl Robertson
8	Syd Howe	18	John Sherf
9	Wally Kilrea	17	Howie Mackie
1	Jimmy Franks	2	Rolly Roulston
3	Bucko McDonald	2	Doug Young C
11	Gord Pettinger		

DETROIT RED WINGS

1942-43 STANLEY CUP CHAMPIONS

Mowers' Masterpiece

After losing the Stanley Cup final in 1941 and 1942, the Red Wings' third straight trip to the final proved to be the charm as they swept the Bruins, avenging the similar treatment they had received from Boston two years earlier.

It would be the last hurrah for Mowers in a Detroit uniform. He joined the Royal Canadian Air Force before the start of post-season scoring mark shared by Grosso and Boston's Bill Cowley.

The 23-year-old Mowers led NHL goalies in wins (25), shutouts (six) and goals-against average (2.47) to win the Vezina Trophy. Selected to the NHL's First All-Star Team, he continued to excel in the playoffs. "There's no doubt who won it for us," Carveth said. "Mowers did.""

armed forces.

A new era in hockey history was ushered in with the 1942-43 season. The departure of the New York Americans franchise left the NHL with the New York Rangers, Boston, Chicago, Detroit, Toronto and Montreal – the so-called "Original Six." **DR**

Mud Bruneteau, always a strong playoff performer, fired a hat-trick in Detroit's 6-2 victory in the series opener. Don Grosso had a three-goal night and goalie Johnny Mowers posted a shutout for a 4-0 verdict in Game 3. Mowers also kept a clean sheet in a 2-0 decision in Game 4. Joe Carveth tallied the Cup-winner and Carl Liscombe's goal was his 14th point of the playoffs, equaling the 1943-44 season and never won another game as a Red Wing.

The only disappointment came when defenseman Jimmy Orlando was arrested by the FBI and charged with draft evasion, accused of falsifying documents suggesting he held an essential war job and was therefore exempt from military service. Convicted, Orlando avoided jail time by enlisting in the Canadian

Semifinals vs. Toronto Maple Leafs

Date	Visitor	Score	Home	Score
Mar. 21	Toronto	2	Detroit	4
Mar. 23	Toronto	3	Detroit	2 (4OT)
Mar. 25	Detroit	4	Toronto	2
Mar. 27	Detroit	3	Toronto	6
Mar. 28	Toronto	2	Detroit	4
Mar. 30	Detroit	3	Toronto	2 (OT)

Detroit won best-of-seven series 4-2

Final vs. Boston Bruins

Date	Visitor	Score	Home	Score
Apr. 1	Boston	2	Detroit	6
Apr. 4	Boston	3	Detroit	4
Apr. 7	Detroit	4	Boston	0
Apr. 8	Detroit	2	Boston	0

Detroit won best-of-seven series 4-0

STANLEY CUP ROSTER
5 Ebbie Goodfellow (Playing Coach)

#	NAME	#	NAME
2	Jack Stewart	15	Cully Simon
4	Jimmy Orlando	10	Don Grosso
12	Sid Abel **C**	7	Carl Liscombe
3	Alex Motter	16	Adam Brown
17	Harry Waston	8	Syd Howe
4	Joe Carveth	18	Les Douglas
9	Mud Bruneteau	5	Harold Jackson
11	Eddie Wares	17	Joe Fisher
1	Johnny Mowers	16	Connie Brown

No way, no Howe

The near-tragic loss of Gordie Howe in the first game of the playoffs could have easily subdued the Red Wings, but they persevered through this and several other challenges to earn their first Stanley Cup since 1943.

Detroit trailed archrival Toronto 3-2 in the semifinal, but rallied, winning Game 7 when defenseman Leo Reise registered the lone goal of the game in the second overtime.

"I never saw a team come back like this one did after Gordie Howe was hurt and we seemed like we were out of the series," Wings coach Tommy Ivan said.

The New York Rangers got the jump on Detroit in the final, also grabbing a 3-2 series edge. Again Detroit rejuvenated and Pete Babando's overtime goal in Game 7 gave the Wings a 4-3 verdict and the title.

"This is one of the great all-time hockey teams," general manager Jack Adams said. "They still won the Cup, even with Gordie Howe out of the lineup. That's like taking a .400 hitter out of the World Series."

Bumped from Madison Square Garden by the circus, the Rangers opted to play Games 2 and 3 in Toronto.

Even without Howe, Detroit managed to capture the Cup in seven games, but without a fight. New York battled Detroit to a 3-3 tie at the end of regulation in Game 7, which Babando ultimately ended at the 28:31 mark of OT. His goal was the first sudden-death tally ever scored in a Game 7 of a final series.

New York's Don Raleigh set a record that would remain unmatched until 1993 when he scored two overtime goals in one Stanley Cup final series. **DR**

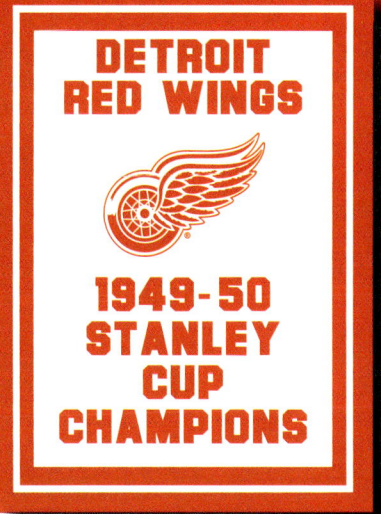

DETROIT RED WINGS

1949-50 STANLEY CUP CHAMPIONS

GORDIE HOWE

BABANDO

Semifinals

Date	Visitor	Score	Home	Score
Mar. 28	Toronto	5	Detroit	0
Mar. 30	Toronto	1	Detroit	3
Apr. 1	Detroit	0	Toronto	2
Apr. 4	Detroit	2	Toronto	1 (2OT)
Apr. 6	Toronto	2	Detroit	0
Apr. 8	Detroit	4	Toronto	0
Apr. 9	Toronto	0	Detroit	1 (OT)

Detroit won best-of-seven series 4-3

Final

Date	Visitor	Score	Home	Score
Apr. 11	NY Rangers	1	Detroit	4
Apr. 13	Detroit	1	NY Rangers	3
Apr. 15	Detroit	4	NY Rangers	0
Apr. 18	NY Rangers	4	Detroit	3 (OT)
Apr. 20	NY Rangers	2	Detroit	1 (OT)
Apr. 22	NY Rangers	0	Detroit	5
Apr. 23	NY Rangers	3	Detroit	4 (2OT)

Detroit won best-of-seven series 4-3

STANLEY CUP ROSTER
Jack Adams (Manager)
Tommy Ivan (Coach)

#	NAME	#	NAME
1	Harry Lumley	10	Jimmy Peters
2	Jack Stewart	15	Marty Pavelich
5	Leo Reise Jr.	16	Jim McFadden
3	Clare Martin	14	Pete Babando
24	Al Dewsbury	11	Max McNab
21	Lee Fogolin	18	Gerry Couture
22	Marcel Pronovost	17	Joe Carveth
4	Red Kelly	19	Steve Black
7	Ted Lindsay	23	Johnny Wilson
12	Sid Abel C	20	Larry Wilson
9	Gordie Howe	27	Doug Mckay
8	George Gee	20	Gord Haidy

Sawchuck takes 8 straight

Detroit established there would be no letdown this spring, opening the semifinals with back-to-back shutout wins over Toronto. The Leafs were victimized 6-2 and 3-1 on home ice and the Wings were on their way to Montreal for the Stanley Cup final.

Terry Sawchuk made his debut in the Cup final and rose to the occasion, recording two shutouts and limiting Montreal to just two goals during the four game series. Meanwhile, Gordie Howe contributed his first two career goals in a Stanley Cup championship series, and the Red Wings set an NHL record by winning all eight postseason games.

After posting 3-1 and 2-1 verdicts at the Montreal Forum, the Wings return to the Olympia where Sawchuk close the door on the Canadiens, and a pair of 3-0 victories brought Lord Stanley's mug back to Hockeytown.

Sawchuk posted an astonishing 0.63 goals-against average and an amazing .977 save percentage. The red light never went on behind him in four games at the Olympia and his four shutouts tied a Stanley Cup record.

Sawchuk's assessment of his Cup performance was, "I never had the idea the puck would get through."

General manager Jack Adams embraced Sawchuk after the Cup-clinching win, saying "The greatest in hockey. It sure helps when you've got a kid like that out there."

The Wings weren't the only ones flying on the ice that spring. So were mollusks, launched from the seats to commence a tradition, which continues today.

When Detroit returned from Montreal up 2-0, Red Wings season-ticket holders Pete and Jerry Cusimano thought it would good luck to toss an octopus on the ice, since its eight tentacles represented the eight wins it took to attain the Stanley Cup.

Acquiring said mollusk would be easy, since the brothers were proprietors of an eastside Detroit fish market.

During the second period of Game 4 of the final, Pete Cusimano reached under his seat and unleashed his octopus, changing Red Wings' playoff hockey forever.

Semifinals

Date	Visitor	Score	Home	Score
Mar. 25	Toronto	0	Detroit	3
Mar. 27	Toronto	0	Detroit	1
Mar. 29	Detroit	6	Toronto	2
Apr. 1	Detroit	3	Toronto	1

Detroit won best-of-seven series 4-0

Final

Date	Visitor	Score	Home	Score
Apr. 10	Detroit	3	Montreal	1
Apr. 12	Detroit	2	Montreal	1
Apr. 13	Montreal	0	Detroit	3
Apr. 15	Montreal	0	Detroit	3

Detroit won best-of-seven series 4-0

STANLEY CUP ROSTER
Jack Adams (Manager)
Tommy Ivan (Coach)

#	NAME	#	NAME
1	Terry Sawchuk	11	Marty Pavelich
2	Bob Goldham	12	Sid Abel C
3	Benny Woit	14	Glen Skov
4	Red Kelly	15	Alex Delvecchio
5	Leo Reise Jr.	17	Johnny Wilson
18	Marcel Pronovost	22	Vic Stasiuk
7	Ted Lindsay	19	Larry Zeidel
8	Tony Leswick		Glen Hall*
9	Gordie Howe		
10	Metro Prystai		*Did not play in playoffs

Haves and Habs nots

One of the most hard-fought finals in Stanley Cup history ended on one of the flukiest Cup-winning goals.

After splitting the first two games at Olympia Stadium, Detroit swept a pair of games at the Montreal Forum and seemed poised to make short work of the defending champion Canadiens. But Montreal had other ideas, winning Games 5 and 6 to send everyone back to the Olympia for a seventh and deciding match.

Floyd Curry gave Montreal a first-period lead, but Red Kelly tied it in the second frame. After a scoreless third period, Tony Leswick's long shot in overtime eluded Montreal goalie Gerry McNeil and gave Detroit the Cup.

"It seemed like an eternity before that red light went on," Wings coach Tommy Ivan said.

The bitterness of the battle was emphasized when Montreal players left the ice before the traditional post-series handshake. "Did you see how they shook hands?" Leswick said. "Not one of them came over."

Gaye Stewart - the player the Wings traded to New York to acquire Leswick in 1951 - was the only Montreal player to later offer congratulations. "If I had shaken hands, I wouldn't have meant it and I refuse to be hypocritical," Canadiens coach Dick Irvin said.

Leswick's Cup-winning tally was only the second goal ever scored in overtime during the seventh and deciding game of a Stanley Cup final series. Leswick, who notched the winner at 4:29 of the first extra period, matched the feat first accomplished by former Red Wings left wing Pete Babando in 1950.

Marguerite Norris, president of the Detroit club, was presented with the Stanley Cup by NHL President Clarence Campbell at the conclusion of the series. She became the first woman in history to have her name engraved on the Stanley Cup.

Semifinal

Date	Visitor	Score	Home	Score
Mar. 23	Toronto	0	Detroit	5
Mar. 25	Toronto	3	Detroit	1
Mar. 27	Detroit	3	Toronto	1
Mar. 30	Detroit	2	Toronto	1
Apr. 1	Toronto	3	Detroit	4 (2OT)

Detroit won best-of-seven series 4-1

Final

Date	Visitor	Score	Home	Score
Apr. 4	Montreal	1	Detroit	3
Apr. 6	Montreal	3	Detroit	1
Apr. 8	Detroit	5	Montreal	2
Apr. 10	Detroit	2	Montreal	0
Apr. 11	Montreal	1	Detroit	0 (OT)
Apr. 13	Detroit	1	Montreal	4
Apr. 16	Montreal	1	Detroit	2 (OT)

Detroit won best-of-seven series 4-3

STANLEY CUP ROSTER

Jack Adams (Manager)
Tommy Ivan (Coach)

#	NAME	#	NAME
1	Terry Sawchuk	15	Alex Delvecchio
4	Red Kelly	10	Metro Prystai
2	Bob Goldham	12	Glen Skov
5	Benny Woit	16	Johnny Wilson
3	Marcel Pronovost	17	Bill Dineen
18	Al Arbour	20	Jimmy Peters
19	Keith Allen	14	Dutch Reibel
7	Ted Lindsay C	21	Gilles Dube
8	Tony Leswick	1	Dave Gatherum*
9	Gordie Howe		*Did not play in playoffs
11	Marty Pavelich		

DETROIT RED WINGS

1954-55 STANLEY CUP CHAMPIONS

Production Line nabs Habs

Few first-year NHL coaches can boast of the success that Jimmy Skinner enjoyed with the 1954-55 Red Wings.

Arriving from Hamilton of the Ontario Hockey Association without any pro coaching experience or NHL playing time, Skinner fell into a difficult position. The Wings were a complacent club who had won the Stanley Cup the spring before and trailed Montreal for first place for much of the season, until closing the campaign with a nine-game winning streak to nip the Habs for top spot.

Skinner showed he wasn't going to take any guff when, during a brawl with Montreal, he exchanged punches with Canadiens captain Butch Bouchard. Later in the season, he told off Clarence Campbell when the NHL president approached the Detroit bench during a game to complain about the players using foul language.

The Red Wings posted a perfect home slate in defending their Stanley Cup crown, sweeping Toronto in the semifinals, then taking Montreal in a seven-game final by winning all four games on Olympia ice. For the first time in a best-of-seven final, the home team won all seven games.

They also established several post-season benchmarks. During a 7-1 rout of the Habs in Game 2, Ted Lindsay collected club records with four goals in the game and four points in one period. Gordie Howe posted his first Stanley Cup hat trick in Game 5 of the final and the line of Lindsay, Howe and Dutch Reibel established a Detroit mark by combining for 51 post-season points. Lindsay's 12 assists tied the mark set by Montreal's Elmer Lach in the 1946 playoffs.

Combined with their nine-game win streak to conclude the regular-season, Detroit won 15 consecutive games before succumbing 4-2 at Montreal in Game 3.

On March 17, Maurice Richard had been suspended for the remainder of the regular-season and playoffs for punching a linesman. The high scoring right winger's absence was sorely felt by the Canadiens.

Howe set two records in the series. He amassed 12 points (five goals, seven assists) in the finals establishing a new mark, and snapping Toe Blake's overall playoff record with 20 points (nine goals, 11 assists) in 11 games.

After retaining the Cup, the Red Wings' rookie bench boss declined to accept the credit. "It scares me to think of all the mistakes I made, right up to the end," Skinner said. "I've been plain lucky." **DR**

Semifinal

Date	Visitor	Score	Home	Score
Mar. 22	Toronto	4	Detroit	7
Mar. 24	Toronto	1	Detroit	2
Mar. 26	Detroit	2	Toronto	1
Mar. 29	Detroit	3	Toronto	0

Detroit won best-of-seven series 4-0

Final

Date	Visitor	Score	Home	Score
Apr. 3	Montreal	2	Detroit	4
Apr. 5	Montreal	1	Detroit	7
Apr. 7	Detroit	2	Montreal	4
Apr. 9	Detroit	3	Montreal	5
Apr. 10	Montreal	1	Detroit	5
Apr. 12	Detroit	3	Montreal	6
Apr. 14	Montreal	1	Detroit	3

Detroit won best-of-seven series 4-3

STANLEY CUP ROSTER
Jack Adams (Manager)
Jimmy Skinner (Coach)

#	NAME	#	NAME
1	Terry Sawchuk	9	Gordie Howe
4	Red Kelly	10	Alex Delvecchio
2	Bob Goldham	11	Marty Pavelich
3	Marcel Pronovost	12	Glen Skov
5	Benny Woit	14	Dutch Reibel
18	Jim Hay	16	Johnny Wilson
15	Larry Hillman	17	Bill Dineen
7	Ted Lindsay **C**	19	Vic Stasiuk
8	Tony Leswick	20	Marcel Bonin

Here's to your future goals.

At Comerica, we're in business to help you succeed. Through great service and flexible financial solutions, our team is dedicated to helping you achieve your goals, both personal and business. If you're looking for an assist with your finances, choose the bank with a full range of products, an unmatched level of responsiveness, and over 150 years of experience. Comerica Bank. We listen. We understand. We make it work.

800-889-2025

We listen. We understand. We make it work.®

ember FDIC. Equal Opportunity Lender.

comerica.com

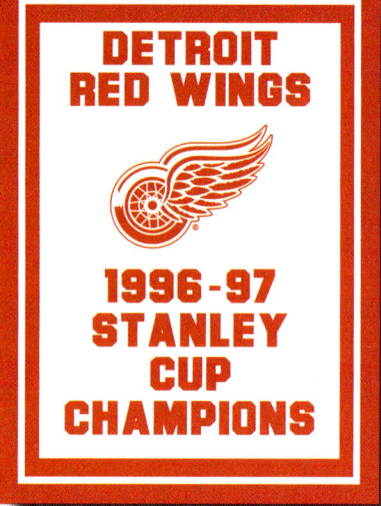

DETROIT RED WINGS

1996-97 STANLEY CUP CHAMPIONS

Finally! Drought ends

Forty-two years of frustration seeped out in a tumultuous ovation from a capacity Joe Louis Arena crowd as the last seconds ticked off the clock in Detroit's 2-1 Stanley Cup-clinching victory over the Philadelphia Flyers.

"I said we'd get it here," Wings Senior Vice President Jimmy Devellano said. "It took us a long time, but we got it here."

The Red Wings swept the Flyers in four games. The series opened at the CoreStates Center in front of 20,291 fans, the largest crowd ever to witness a hockey game in the state of Pennsylvania.

Goalie Mike Vernon made 26 saves in a 4-2 Detroit win as unheralded Kirk Maltby and Joe Kocur gave Detroit a 2-1 lead after the first period. Sergei Fedorov tallied the game-winner just after the midway point of the second. Maltby scored again in Game 2, breaking a 2-2 tie in the second period with what would prove to be the game-winning goal.

The Red Wings returned home to a vocal and supportive crowd for Game 3 at Joe Louis Arena and responded with a 6-1 win to take a commanding 3-0 series lead. Down a goal, Detroit replied with three unanswered goals before the period ended. The win snapped Detroit's eight game and 33-year home ice losing streaks in the Stanley Cup final. Fedorov and Martin Lapointe each tallied twice to pace the Red Wings.

The Red Wings completed the series sweep by defeating the Flyers 2-1 in Game 4. Defenseman Nicklas Lidstrom's goal late in the first period gave Detroit a lead it would not relinquish and Darren McCarty scored the Stanley Cup winning goal on a spectacular individual effort in the second period.

The roar reached its peak when captain Steve Yzerman hoisted the shiny, silver mug over his head.

"The majority of this team played in the Stanley Cup final two years ago," Yzerman said. "You realize that finishing second means absolutely nothing."

Scotty Bowman, who coached his seventh Cup winner, praised the determination of his team.

"This team went through a lot of agony the last two years and sometimes I think you have to take that pill to learn what you have to do to win," Bowman said.

Vernon was named the Conn Smythe winner as the MVP of the playoffs, finishing the postseason with a 16-4 record and a 1.76 goals-against average. He allowed two goals or fewer in 17 of 20 playoff games.

Conference Quarterfinals

Date	Visitor	Score	Home	Score
Apr. 16	St. Louis	2	Detroit	0
Apr. 18	St. Louis	1	Detroit	2
Apr. 20	Detroit	3	St. Louis	2
Apr. 22	Detroit	0	St. Louis	4
Apr. 25	St. Louis	2	Detroit	5
Apr. 27	Detroit	3	St. Louis	1

Detroit won best-of-seven series 4-2

Conference Semifinals

Date	Visitor	Score	Home	Score
May 2	Anaheim	1	Detroit	2 (OT)
May 4	Anaheim	2	Detroit	3 (3OT)
May 6	Detroit	5	Anaheim	3
May 8	Detroit	3	Anaheim	2 (2OT)

Detroit won best-of-seven series 4-0

Conference Finals

Date	Visitor	Score	Home	Score
May 15	Detroit	1	Colorado	2
Mat 17	Detroit	4	Colorado	2
May 19	Colorado	1	Detroit	2
May 22	Colorado	0	Detroit	6
May 24	Detroit	0	Colorado	6
May 26	Colorado	1	Detroit	3

Detroit won best-of-seven series 4-2

Final

Date	Visitor	Score	Home	Score
May 31	Detroit	4	Philadelphia	2
June 3	Detroit	4	Philadelphia	2
June 5	Philadelphia	1	Detroit	6
June 7	Philadelphia	1	Detroit	2

Detroit won best-of-seven series 4-0

STANLEY CUP ROSTER

Scotty Bowman (Coach)
Barry Smith (Associate Coach)
Dave Lewis (Associate Coach)
Mike Krushelnyski (Assistant Coach)

#	NAME	#	NAME
19	Steve Yzerman C	5	Nicklas Lidstrom
17	Doug Brown	18	Kirk Maltby
11	Mathieu Dandenault	25	Darren McCarty
33	Kris Draper	55	Larry Murphy
91	Sergei Fedorov	30	Chris Osgood
2	Viacheslav Fetisov	4	Jamie Pushor
31	Kevin Hodson	3	Bob Rouse
15	Tomas Holmstrom	28	Tomas Sandstrom
26	Joe Kocur	14	Brendan Shanahan
16	Vladimir Konstantinov	37	Tim Taylor
13	Vyacheslav Kozlov	29	Mike Vernon
20	Martin Lapointe	27	Aaron Ward
8	Igor Larionov		

2007-08 STANLEY CUP CHAMPIONS

Win one for Vladdy

With a four game sweep of the Washington Capitals, the Red Wings became the first team since Pittsburgh (1991 and '92) to repeats as Stanley Cup champs. The Wings were led by Steve Yzerman, who became just the fifth player to receive the Conn Smythe Trophy as the most valuable player in the playoff while captain of his team. He also set a club record with 18 assists and 24 points. Scotty Bowman equaled Toe Blake's NHL record of eight Stanley Cup coaching victories.

"We found a lot of ways to play," Bowman said. "We found a lot of ways to win. This team was totally focused on the mission."

Despite the series sweep, Detroit did not have a smooth road to the Cup, as they were forced to play six games in each of the three series leading up to the finals. Overall, the team had equal success at home and on the road, posting identical 8-3 records. A total of 10 Red Wings players contributed the 16 game-winning goals scored en route to the Stanley Cup.

The on-ice celebration produced one of the most emotional moments in NHL history, as injured teammate Vladimir Konstantinov participated in the post-game festivities from his wheelchair. Konstantinov was a key part of Detroit's Stanley Cup title in 1997, but nearly lost his life in a car accident one week after the '97 victory.

As emotional as Detroit's 1997 Stanley Cup victory was for long-suffering Wings' fans, the '98 triumph melted even the coldest of hearts.

When Konstantinov was wheeled onto the ice after Detroit's 4-1 Cup-clinching win at the MCI Center, the sentiment of the moment took over. "This is so emotional, it's great," Igor Larionov said as he helped Konstantinov take a victory lap in his wheelchair with the Cup. "This is for Vladdy and Sergei (Mnatsakanov)."

"We found a lot of ways to play," Bowman said. "We found a lot of ways to win. This team was totally focused on the mission."

And they never stopped believing

DETROIT RED WINGS 1997-98 STANLEY CUP CHAMPIONS

Conference Quarterfinals

Date	Visitor	Score	Home	Score
Apr. 22	Phoenix	3	Detroit	6
Apr. 24	Phoenix	7	Detroit	4
Apr. 26	Detroit	2	Phoenix	3
Apr. 28	Detroit	4	Phoenix	2
Apr. 30	Phoenix	1	Detroit	3
May 3	Detroit	5	Phoenix	3

Detroit win best-of-seven series 4-2

Conference Semifinals

Date	Visitor	Score	Home	Score
May 8	St. Louis	4	Detroit	2
May 10	St. Louis	1	Detroit	6
May 12	Detroit	3	St. Louis	2 (2OT)
May 14	Detroit	5	St. Louis	2
May 17	St. Louis	3	Detroit	1
May 19	Detroit	6	St. Louis	1

Detroit won best-of-seven series 4-2

Conference Finals

Date	Visitor	Score	Home	Score
May 24	Detroit	2	Dallas	0
May 26	Detroit	1	Dallas	3
May 29	Dallas	3	Detroit	5
May 31	Dallas	2	Detroit	3
June 3	Detroit	2	Dallas	3 (OT)
June 5	Dallas	0	Detroit	2

Detroit won best-of-seven series 4-2

Final

Date	Visitor	Score	Home	Score
June 9	Washington	1	Detroit	2
June 11	Washington	4	Detroit	5
June 13	Detroit	2	Washington	1
June 16	Detroit	4	Washington	1

Detroit won best-of-seven series 4-0

STANLEY CUP ROSTER

Scotty Bowman (Coach)
Barry Smith (Associate Coach)
Dave Lewis (Associate Coach)
Jim Bedard (Goaltending Consultant)

#	NAME	#	NAME
19	Steve Yzerman C	20	Martin Lapointe
17	Doug Brown	8	Igor Larionov
11	Mathieu Dandenault	5	Nicklas Lidstrom
33	Kris Draper	34	Jamie Macoun
44	Anders Eriksson	18	Kirk Maltby
91	Sergei Fedorov	25	Darren McCarty
2	Viacheslav Fetisov	15	Dmitri Mironov
41	Brent Gilchrist	55	Larry Murphy
31	Kevin Hodson	30	Chris Osgood
96	Tomas Holmstrom	3	Bob Rouse
22	Mike Knuble	14	Brendan Shanahan
26	Joe Kocur	27	Aaron Ward
13	Vyacheslav Kozlov		

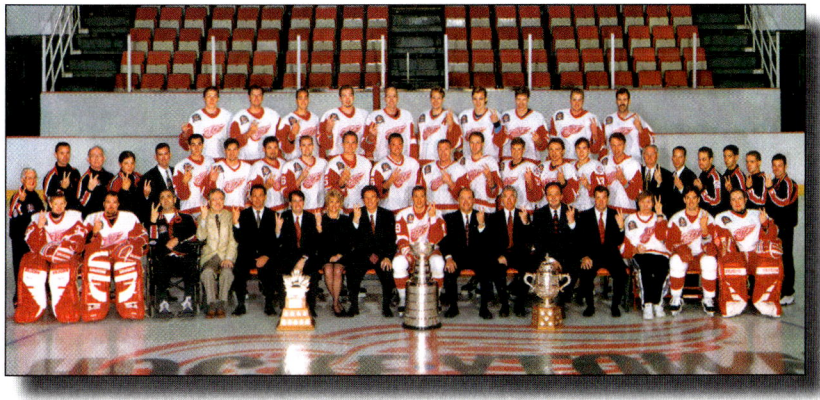

2007-08 STANLEY CUP CHAMPIONS

Bowman's Finale

DETROIT RED WINGS
2001-02 STANLEY CUP CHAMPIONS

The Red Wings became the first team in NHL history to win the Stanley Cup after starting the playoffs with two losses at home. Dropping the first two games in the conference quarterfinals to the Vancouver Canucks, the Red Wings rebounded, winning 16 of the next 21 games en route to their third championship under legendary coach Scotty Bowman, who established a new coaching record with his ninth Cup victory, surpassing the mark once held by Montreal coach Toe Blake.

After skating around the Joe Louis Arena ice surface, Bowman announced that he was hanging hung them up for good.

"I just coached my last game," Bowman said moments after the Cup was acquired. "I made up my mind in February. I know it's time now."

Bowman finished his career with an NHL-record 1,244 regular season wins. His playoff (227) and Cup final (36) win totals are also league marks.

After the slow start against the Canucks, Detroit proceeded to win the series in six games. They then defeated the St. Louis Blues in five games before eliminating the Colorado Avalanche in a classic seven-game conference final series.

Those series wins set up a Stanley Cup match against the Eastern Conference champion Carolina Hurricanes. The Hurricanes stunned the Red Wings in Game 1 on the strength of Ron Francis' overtime goal. It was Carolina's only win in the series as the Red Wings won four straight, including a triple overtime win in Game 3 that proved to be the turning point in the series. The Cup win was a first for many veterans on the team, including goalie Dominik Hasek, forward Luc Robitaille, and defensemen Steve Duchesne and Fredrik Olausson. It also marked the second Cup win for defenseman Chris Chelios, 16 years after he first won the Cup as a member of the Montreal Canadiens in 1986.

Conference Quarterfinals

Date	Visitor	Score	Home	Score
Apr. 17	Vancouver	4	Detroit	3 (OT)
Apr. 19	Vancouver	5	Detroit	2
Apr. 21	Detroit	3	Vancouver	1
Apr. 23	Detroit	4	Vancouver	2
Apr. 25	Vancouver	0	Detroit	4
Apr. 27	Detroit	6	Vancouver	4

Detroit won best-of-seven series 4-2

Conference Semifinals

Date	Visitor	Score	Home	Score
May 2	St. Louis	0	Detroit	2
May 4	St. Louis	2	Detroit	3
May 7	Detroit	1	St. Louis	6
May 9	Detroit	4	St. Louis	3
May 11	St. Louis	0	Detroit	4

Detroit won best-of-seven series 4-1

Conference Finals

Date	Visitor	Score	Home	Score
May 18	Colorado	3	Detroit	5
May 20	Colorado	4	Detroit	3
May 22	Detroit	2	Colorado	1
May 25	Detroit	2	Colorado	3
May 27	Colorado	2	Detroit	1
May 29	Detroit	2	Colorado	0
May 31	Colorado	0	Detroit	7

Detroit won best-of-seven series 4-3

Final

Date	Visitor	Score	Home	Score
June 4	Carolina	3	Detroit	2 (OT)
June 6	Carolina	1	Detroit	3
June 8	Detroit	3	Carolina	2 (3OT)
June 10	Detroit	3	Carolina	0
June 13	Carolina	1	Detroit	3

Detroit won best-of-seven series 4-1

STANLEY CUP ROSTER

Scotty Bowman (Coach)
Barry Smith (Associate Coach)
Dave Lewis (Associate Coach)
Jim Bedard (Goaltending Consultant)

#	NAME	#	NAME
19	Steve Yzerman C	17	Brett Hull
24	Chris Chelios	8	Igor Larionov
11	Matheiu Dandenault	34	Manny Legace
13	Pavel Datsyuk	5	Nicklas Lidstrom
21	Boyd Devereaux	18	Kirk Maltby
33	Kris Draper	25	Darren McCarty
28	Steve Duchesne	27	Fredrik Olausson
91	Sergei Fedorov	20	Luc Robitaille
2	Jiri Fischer	14	Brendan Shanahan
39	Dominik Hasek	71	Jiri Slegr
96	Tomas Holmstrom	29	Jason Williams

2007-08 STANLEY CUP CHAMPIONS

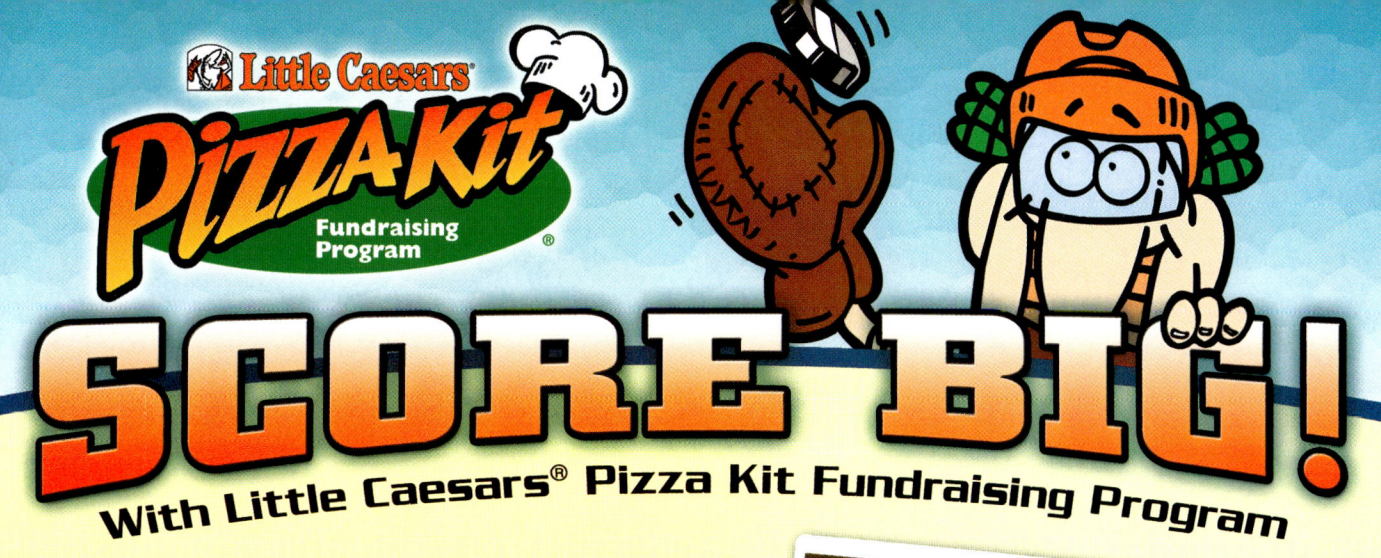

SCORE BIG!
With Little Caesars® Pizza Kit Fundraising Program

Little Caesars® Pizza Kit Fundraising Program is a great way to raise **BIG!BIG! DOUGH** for your team uniforms, ice time and tournaments!

WHAT MAKES LITTLE CAESARS® PIZZA KIT FUNDRAISING PROGRAM A WINNER?

BIG!BIG! PROFIT – Earn up to **$7.25** per item sold!

FREE DELIVERY – Chances are we are in your neighborhood every week!

EASY & CONVENIENT – We'll make sure your fundraiser is **EASY** and your delivery is accurate and on time.

LITTLE CAESARS® QUALITY – We choose all of our ingredients on the basis of quality, taste and nutritional value. Ingredients in our Pizza Kit products include vitamins A & C, bone building calcium, complex carbohydrates and protein.

CALL US TODAY!
1-888-4-LC-KITS (1-888-452-5487)
or visit **PizzaKit.com**

Earn Up To $7.25 Per Kit Sold!

All the ingredients to make wholesome and delicious pizza at home in less than 10 minutes!

Profit structure applies to your area and may vary in other areas of the U.S. Minimum items required for FREE delivery.

DETROIT RED WINGS
REGULAR SEASON REVIEW

OCTOBER

OCT. 3 — RED WINGS 3, DUCKS 2 (SO): Jiri Hudler scored the only shootout goal in the season-opening rematch of last spring's Western Conference finals. Anaheim opened the season in England, where it split two games with LA.

OCT. 6 — BLACKHAWKS 4, RED WINGS 3 (SO): Patrick Kane scored the only goal in the shootout, lifting the Hawks, who trailed 3-1 entering the third. Brian Rafalski and Nicklas Lidstrom each had a goal and an assist.

OCT. 8 — RED WINGS 4, OILERS 2: Chris Chelios, the NHL's oldest active player at 45, skated in his 1,550th game. Mikael Samuelsson had a goal and an assist.

OCT. 10 — RED WINGS 4, FLAMES 2: Chris Osgood won his season debut, stopping 18 shots. Henrik Zetterberg scored the team's sixth power-play goal and got his eighth point of the season.

OCT. 12 — BLACKHAWKS 3, RED WINGS 2: Robert Lang scores the game-winning goal, capping the comeback. Zetterberg extended his home scoring streak to 20 games, dating back to last season.

OCT. 14 — RED WINGS 4, KINGS 1: Zetterberg had a goal and two assists. Osgood made 27 saves in his 600th career start, and second of the season.

OCT. 15 — DUCKS 6, RED WINGS 3: Kris Draper, Zetterberg and Rafalski scored. Draper extended his goal-scoring streak to a career-best five straight games.

OCT. 18 — RED WINGS 4, SHARKS 2: Matt Ellis scored his first NHL goal on a no-look backhander in the third, helping secure the comeback win. Osgood made 23 saves as the Red Wings earned their fourth win in six games.

2007-08 STANLEY CUP CHAMPIONS

DETROIT RED WINGS
SEASON REVIEW

OCT. 20 – RED WINGS 5, COYOTES 2: Kirk Maltby had a pair of second-period goals and Zetterberg added a goal and an assist. For the Wings, it's their fifth straight win in Phoenix dating back to January 24, 2004.

OCT. 24 – RED WINGS 3, CANUCKS 2: Ellis scored his second goal of the season, and Holmstrom and Zetterberg both scored en route to the win over the visiting Canucks.

OCT. 26 – RED WINGS 5, SHARKS 1: Valtteri Filppula and Andreas Lilja scored their first goals of the season, and Zetterberg continued his season-long scoring streak.

OCT. 28 – RED WINGS 3, CANUCKS 2: Hudler scored a highlight-reel goal in the final minute of the second period, and linemates Samuelsson and Filppula combined on another tally late in the first, lifting Detroit in the first of a three-game trip through western Canada.

OCT 30 – RED WINGS 2, OILERS 1: Filppula scored with just 24.4 seconds left in regulation to give the Wings their sixth straight win.

NOVEMBER

NOV. 1 – RED WINGS 4, FLAMES 1: Zetterberg scored his league-leading 11th and 12th goals, helping Detroit take all three games of its western Canada trip for the first time in 21 attempts. Osgood made 26 saves to improve his mark to 7-0.

NOV. 7 – RED WINGS 3, PREDATORS 2 (SO): Pavel Datsyuk and Zetterberg scored in the shootout to end Nashville's comeback bid. Osgood improves to 8-0, his best start in 14 seasons.

NOV. 9 – RED WINGS 4, BLUE JACKETS 1: Detroit got a pair of power-play goals from Dan Cleary and Holmstrom, and goalie Dominik Hasek made 15 saves in his return after a five-game absence. It was the Wings' ninth straight win, which tied a franchise mark.

NOV. 11 – BLACKHAWKS 3, RED WINGS 2: Zetterberg picked up another assist, moving his season-opening point streak to 17 games, the longest streak in franchise history. However, Osgood's 20 game point streak, which began in January 2007, ended.

NOV. 13 – BLUES 4, RED WINGS 3: Datsyuk, Cleary and Filppula scored for Detroit, who lost the lead in the second period despite holding a 17-7 shots advantage in the period

NOV. 17 – BLACKHAWKS 5, RED WINGS 3: The Blackhawks continued their early-season dominance of the Red Wings, despite goals from Rafalski, Holmstrom and Zetterberg. Chicago scored three goals in the third.

NOV. 18 – RED WINGS 5, BLUE JACKETS 4 (SO): Johan Franzen scored the winning shootout goal in the fifth round of the tiebreaker and Detroit snapped a three-game losing skid. Lidstrom had a goal and two assists in the Wings' comeback win.

NOV. 21 – RED WINGS 3, BLUES 0: Osgood earned his first shutout since March 1, 2006, the 44th of his career, ranking fifth among active goalies. Cleary netted the game-winning goal.

NOV. 22 – PREDATORS 3, RED WINGS 2: Despite power-play goals from Franzen and Zetterberg, the Wings struggled on Thanksgiving. Hasek took the loss, his third straight.

NOV. 24 – BLUE JACKETS 3, RED WINGS 2 (SO): Holmstrom and Datsyuk scored just five-seconds apart in the second. The goals set a club record for fastest two goals scored, besting the previous mark (seven-seconds), accomplished in 1936 and '87.

NOV. 27 – RED WINGS 5, FLAMES 3: Quick goals again make the difference as Datsyuk and Draper scored just 23-seconds apart. And one day after Osgood turned 35, he earned the win, helping Detroit improve to 7-0 against Northwest Division foes.

NOV. 29 – RED WINGS 4, LIGHTNING 2: Tomas Kopecky scored the game-winning goal in his first game back from a shoulder injury. Osgood stopped 19 shots in Detroit's first game of the season against an Eastern Conference opponent.

DECEMBER

DEC. 1 – RED WINGS 3, COYOTES 2: Cleary's power-play goal completed Detroit's third-period comeback. Zetterberg had a goal and an assist, Datsyuk also scored, and Rafalski had two assists. Osgood made 24 saves.

DEC. 4 – RED WINGS 4, CANADIENS 1: Datsyuk scored two unassisted goals off turnovers and Hasek stopped 15 shots. Niklas Kronwall and Zetterberg also scored. Gordie Howe, Ted Lindsay, Alex Delvecchio, Marcel Pronovost and Marcel Dionne were present as the Canadiens honored their long-standing rivalry with Detroit in a pre-game ceremony.

DEC. 7 – RED WINGS 5, WILD 0: Zetterberg had his second career hat trick and Hasek stopped 19 shots for his 77th career shutout. Franzen added a goal and an assist, and Hudler also scored. Datsyuk added three assists.

DEC. 9 – RED WINGS 5, HURRICANES 2: Detroit delivered the deciding punch in a four goal, 12-minute span of the second period. Hudler had an assist on each of Detroit's first three goals.

DEC. 10 – RED WINGS 2, PREDATORS 1: Kopecky and Filppula scored first-period goals, lifting Detroit to its seventh straight win. Osgood stopped 30 shots.

DEC. 13 – OILERS 4, RED WINGS 3 (SO): Zetterberg scored twice, and in only his second game since being called up, center Mark Hartigan also tallied in the losing cause.

DEC. 15 – RED WINGS 5, PANTHERS 2: Mike Babcock got his 200th career NHL coaching win. Filppula scored on a penalty shot, and Cleary scored the game-winner.

2007-08 STANLEY CUP CHAMPIONS

DETROIT RED WINGS
REGULAR SEASON REVIEW

JAN. 12 – SENATORS 3, RED WINGS 2: A meeting of the top teams from each conference went to the East. Rafalski scored on a power play, and Hudler evened it at 2-2 when he jumped on a rebound.

JAN. 15 – THRASHERS 5, RED WINGS 1: Hasek replaced Osgood, but it wasn't enough to overcome a Marian Hossa hat trick. It's the Wings' second straight loss to an Eastern Conference team.

JAN. 17 – RED WINGS 3, CANUCKS 2 (SO): Zetterberg scored on Detroit's second shootout attempt, deking once before slipping the puck five-hole on Roberto Luongo. Cleary scored both regulation goals.

DEC. 17 – RED WINGS 4, CAPITALS 3 (SO): Detroit improved to 5-0 against Eastern Conference teams when Datsyuk, Zetterberg and Hudler all chose to go with (successful) backhand shots in the shootout.

DEC. 19 – RED WINGS 6, KINGS 2: Kronwall had a career-high four assists and six different Wings scored en route to a win over the league's worst team.

DEC. 20 – BLUES 3, RED WINGS 2: The loss ended the Red Wings' 12-game point streak. Zetterberg picked up an assist, giving the Swedish star 50 points for the season.

DEC. 22 – RED WINGS 4, WILD 1: Detroit had a season-high 51 shots, the most ever allowed by the Wild at home. Lidstrom's lob pass to Cleary for a breakaway goal was the 900th point of Lidstrom's NHL career.

DEC. 26 – RED WINGS 5, BLUES 0: Filppula had his first career two-goal game, and Osgood stopped 20 shots for his 45th career shutout. Rafalski added a goal and two assists.

DEC. 27 – RED WINGS 4, AVALANCHE 2: Filppula scored two goals for the second straight game, and Hasek made 22 saves. Hudler broke a 2-2 tie with nine-minutes left in the second.

DEC. 29 – RED WINGS 4, COYOTES 2: Datsyuk scored with just over four minutes remaining in regulation to break a tie. Samuelsson scored in his second straight game, and third in his last five.

DEC. 31 – BLUES 2, RED WINGS 0: It was the first time since 1998 that the Wings lost on New Year's Eve. It's also the fist time that the Wings are shutout this season.

JANUARY

JAN. 2 – RED WINGS 4, STARS 1: With its 30th win, Detroit set its best first-half record ever. Zetterberg (back spasms), who missed the previous five games, returned to assist on two goals, and Aaron Downey got his first point of the season.

JAN. 5 – RED WINGS 3, STARS 0: Hasek stopped 22 shots for his 78th career shutout, and Rafalski scored a first-period goal. Hasek also reached 375 victories to break a tie with John Vanbiesbrouck for 11th place on the all-time career list.

JAN. 6 – RED WINGS 3, BLACKHAWKS 1: Zetterberg, Cleary and Samuelsson scored in the first, lifting Detroit over Chicago for the first time this season.

JAN. 8 – RED WINGS 1, AVALANCHE 0: The win was Hasek's 79th career shutout and third this season. Chelios becomes the second oldest NHL player of all time, passing Moe Roberts. At 45 years and 348 days, Chelios is only second to Gordie Howe.

JAN. 10 – WILD 6, RED WINGS 5 (SO): The combined 10 goals represented the most at JLA this season. Drake scored a shorthanded goal, Kronwall also scored, but Marian Gaborik's shootout goal was the difference.

JAN. 19 – RED WINGS 6, SAN JOSE 3: Draper scored a short-handed goal, and Lidstrom and Holmstrom added power-play tallies in a penalty-filled second that helped the Wings open their annual father-son road trip.

JAN. 22 – RED WINGS 3, KINGS 0: Osgood got his 46th career shutout, stopping all 27 shots. It's Osgood's 356th career win, lifting him past Rogie Vachon for 15th place on the career list. Holmstrom, Samuelsson and Franzen all scored.

JAN. 23 – RED WINGS 2, DUCKS 1: Hasek made 24 saves, and Rafalski and Filppula scored. Detroit held the Ducks to 25 shots on its way to winning the ninth road game in 10 tries.

JAN. 30 – RED WINGS 3, COYOTES 2: Datsyuk assisted on all three goals, extending his point streak to four games. Lidstrom netted the game-winner in the third in another comeback victory.

2007-08 STANLEY CUP CHAMPIONS

YOUR EXTRA MAN ADVANTAGE

State Farm® agents come to play, delivering breakaway personal service and discounts up to 40%. No wonder State Farm has more fans than any other car insurance company. Join the winning team today.

statefarm.com®

LIKE A GOOD NEIGHBOR  STATE FARM IS THERE.®

State Farm Mutual Automobile Insurance Company, State Farm Indemnity Company • Bloomington, IL

FEBRUARY

FEB. 1 — RED WINGS 2, AVALANCHE 0: Zetterberg's 30th goal of the season helped Detroit beat the Avs for the third time this season. Hasek earned his 80th career shutout, fourth of the season -- and second against Colorado.

FEB. 2 — RED WINGS 3, BRUINS 1: Datsyuk scored the tiebreaking goal early in the third. Osgood made 22 saves and the Red Wings bottled up Boston over the second half for their 40th win.

FEB. 5 — RED WINGS 3, WILD 2 (OT): Cleary tied it with 1:20 to go in regulation and Brett Lebda scored 1:37 into overtime, completing the come-from-behind win.

FEB. 7 — KINGS 5, RED WINGS 3: Zetterberg scored twice, but the Wings could not fend off a third period rally, snapping their eight-game winning streak.

FEB. 9 — MAPLE LEAFS 3, RED WINGS 2 (OT): Lidstrom tied it 1-1 with a deflection of Datsyuk's pass in the second. Samuelsson gave Detroit a lead slapping in a rebound. Cleary suffered a broken jaw when he was hit in the face by a puck.

FEB. 10 — DUCKS 3, RED WINGS 2: It seemed like Lidstrom tied the game with 40-seconds left in regulation, but the goal was waved off when Holmstrom interfered with the goalie. Franzen scored a power-play goal in the third.

FEB. 12 — PREDATORS 4, RED WINGS 2: The Predators struck quickly with three first-period goals on four shots. Osgood was pulled in favor of Jimmy Howard. Zetterberg ended a seven-game points streak.

FEB. 15 — BLUE JACKETS 5, RED WINGS 1: For the second straight game, Howard entered in relief, and the Wings dropped their fifth straight game. Datsyuk scored Detroit's lone goal.

FEB. 17 — STARS 1, RED WINGS 0: Howard stopped 30 shots, playing in his fourth career start. Babcock also switched up the lines in an attempt to spark his struggling team, but the Wings fell to 0-5-1 in their last six.

FEB. 18 — RED WINGS 4, AVALANCHE 0: The Wings were steaming over a hit that left Lidstrom with a knee injury. Downey administered on-ice justice when he went after culprit Ian Laperriere later in the period.

FEB. 22 — FLAMES 1, RED WINGS 0: Miikka Kiprusoff was at his best in the third, stopping 13 shots in the period. Twice the Red Wings hit a goalpost in the final 20 minutes. Osgood made 25 saves.

FEB. 23 — CANUCKS 4, RED WINGS 1: With Hasek nursing a hip injury and Osgood playing the previous night, Howard got the start. He made a couple of great stops early and finished with 31 saves. Datsyuk scored for Detroit.

FEB. 26 — OILERS 4, RED WINGS 3 (SO): Jonathan Ericsson scored his first career goal. Datsyuk and Filppula also scored. Detroit was scoreless in shootout, and lost for the ninth time in 10 games.

FEB. 29 — SHARKS 3, RED WINGS 2: Brad Stuart made his debut with Detroit, and injured Kronwall and Hasek made their returns to the lineup. Zetterberg and Samuelsson both scored power-play goals.

MARCH

MAR. 2 — RED WINGS 4, SABRES 2: Franzen and Filppula each had a goal and assist, and Hasek made 22 saves against his former team. It was the first time Detroit played in Buffalo since Dec. 10, 2003.

MAR. 5 — RED WINGS 4, BLUES 1: Rafalski was back in the lineup and scored his first goal in more than a month. Datsyuk also scored twice and Hasek made 18 saves.

MAR. 9 — RED WINGS 4, PREDATORS 3: Franzen notched two goals, including the game-winner in the second. It's his third straight game-winning goal — the longest stretch of his career.

MAR. 11 — RED WINGS 3, BLACKHAWKS 1: Playing in his 1,000th career game, Drake reaches another milestone when he registers career assist No. 300. Maltby, Datsyuk and Franzen also scored.

MAR. 13 — RED WINGS 5, STARS 3: The win gave Detroit 100-points for an NHL record-tying eighth straight season. Datsyuk scored twice and added an assist, while extending his point streak to eight games.

MAR. 15 — PREDATORS 3, RED WINGS 1: Kronwall scored the only goal for Detroit who saw its five-game winning streak come to an end.

REGULAR SEASON REVIEW

MARCH

MAR. 16 – BLUE JACKETS 4, RED WINGS 3: Franzen scored two power-play goals. Kopecky also had a goal. Hasek was pulled in the second after allowing four goals on 10 shots.

MAR. 19 – RED WINGS 3, BLUE JACKETS 1: Zetterberg's hat trick was the difference with all three goals in the third period. It was his third career three-goal performance, and he tied his single-season best for goals (39).

MAR. 20 – RED WINGS 6, PREDATORS 3: Franzen's third-period goal broke a tie. Kronwall, Chelios and Rafalski each scored second-period goals, and Datsyuk added a pair of late insurance tallies. Hasek earned his 385th victory, tying him for 10th place with Mike Vernon.

MAR. 22 – RED WINGS 4, BLUE JACKETS 1: Datsyuk set up power-play goals by Lidstrom and Zetterberg, and then also scored a short-handed tally, helping Detroit to its 50th win of the season.

MAR. 25 – RED WINGS 2, BLUES 1: Franzen scored his 11th goal in as many games, and Zetterberg added his 150th career goal. Osgood made 17 saves for the Red Wings, who have won nine of the last 11, outscoring opponents, 39-23.

MAR. 28 – BLUES 4, RED WINGS 3 (OT): Franzen scored twice and Rafalski added another. Zetterberg and Datsyuk each had three assists, and Osgood stopped 17 shots.

MAR. 30 – RED WINGS 1, PREDATORS 0 (OT): Celebrating his 80th birthday, Gordie Howe watched Franzen break one of his franchise records when Franzen scored his sixth game-winning goal in March. Howe's mark for most game-winning goals in a month stood since February 1952.

APRIL

APR. 2 – BLACKHAWKS 6, RED WINGS 2: Zetterberg and Maltby scored, but it was too little, too late as Chicago tallied three times on its first six shots.

APR. 3 – RED WINGS 3, BLUE JACKETS 2: Zetterberg scored from behind the net with 11.4 seconds left lifting the Wings to a come-from-behind win that wrapped up the club's sixth Presidents' Trophy.

APR. 6 – RED WINGS 4, BLACKHAWKS 1: Lidstrom scored two power-play goals, while Hudler and Hartigan also tallied. Detroit claimed the Jennings Trophy — given annually to the team with the lowest overall goals against. Detroit allowed just 184 goals.

THANK YOU!

THE DETROIT RED WINGS WOULD LIKE TO THANK THEIR CORPORATE SPONSORS FOR THEIR SUPPORT DURING THE 2007-08 SEASON

GO RED WINGS!

JANUARY 8, 2008

Wings' trio pegged as All-Star starters

By Bill Roose

The Red Wings' hot first half start to the season was rewarded by the fans with an NHL-best three starters named to this season's All-Star Game in Atlanta on Jan. 27.

Led by five-time Norris Trophy winner Nicklas Lidstrom, who is making his 10th appearance and eighth start, the Wings will also have center Pavel Datsyuk and left wing Henrik Zetterberg in the starting lineup for the Western Conference at Philips Arena.

It's the first time since 2002 that the Wings have been represented by at least three starters in the All-Star Game. In the old World vs. North America forward, the Wings' starters were Lidstrom, Dominik Hasek, Brendan Shanahan and Sergei Fedorov. Defenseman Chris Chelios also played in that game.

The Wings' mark for most players in an all-star game is six, done in 1951, 1953 and 1957.

The Western squad will be led this month by coach Mike Babcock, who earned the honor by way of the Wings' best overall record through the first 41 games.

"It's a good honor for them," Babcock said. "They're real good players and it's a real special honor and they earned it. The big thing here, obviously, is I'm going because they're going. It's straight forward."

The league's hockey operations department, in conjunction with league general managers, will round out the complete All-Star rosters, which will be announced on Thursday (Western Conference) and Friday (Eastern Conference).

It's possible that the Wings could add two more players to the Western roster with goalie Chris Osgood and defenseman Brian Rafalski. Osgood, who has a 19-2-1 record, continues to lead the league in goals against average (1.68) and save percentage (.932).

Rafalski has been a tremendous performer -- especially in the power play -- since joining the Wings as a free agent during the off-season. He's second among defensemen in scoring with 36 points. He also ranks fourth in league power play points with 21.

The Wings entered Tuesday's home game against the Colorado Avalanche with a league-best 32-8-3 record for 67 points.

Detroit boasts one of the best special teams units in the league. They are ranked second in power plays, having scored 46 goals in 197 chances (23.4 percent). The Wings are also fifth at killing penalties, allowing 27 goals on 199 situations (86.4 percent).

Individually, Zetterberg and Datsyuk are in the top 10 amongst scoring forwards with 54 and 52 points respectively. Lidstrom is tops among defenseman with 40 points and leads the league with a plus-34 rating.

"The thing with this league is that you have to keep getting better and better," Babcock said. "Those guys have had real good starts for us and we've had a number of other guys who have had good starts, and ideally we'll be able to keep it going."

For Lidstrom, the three starters heading to Atlanta is an indication of

how well the season has gone from a team standpoint under Babcock's tutelage.

"It goes to tell that the team has played real well in the first half of the season," he said. "We're all honored and proud to be going to the All-Star Game.

"It's a tremendous honor for (Babcock) as well and I think he's just happy to get a chance to meet some of the best players in the world and coach some of the best players in the world, too. It'll be fun for him too."

While NHL success is more often measured in Stanley Cup titles, receiving individual acknowledgement from the fans is never overlooked.

"I'm proud to go and I'm glad that the fans appreciate what I do and it's going to be a few exciting days down there," said Zetterberg, who is making his first All-Star appearance.

Datsyuk is making his second All-Star appearance, having played in the 2004 game in Minnesota for then-Wings coach Dave Lewis.

"The first time I didn't speak English well and it wasn't that comfortable," Datsyuk said. "I have more experience and speak more English now. I'm happy. It's more comfortable for me and I think we'll have a good time in Atlanta. It's a good surprise; a good (Russian) Christmas."

Zetterberg, who missed last year's game in Dallas with a sore back, is thrilled at the opportunity to play this season's exhibition game.

"It's going to be exciting," he said. "It's always nice to have (Datsyuk) with me, it makes it a lot easier for me out on the ice.

"I don't think there's a whole lot of pressure to go down there. Just be yourself and have a lot of fun and enjoy those days. You have enough pressure when you're playing in the regular-season, so those few days, go down there and just relax and enjoy your stay."

2007-2008
THE PLAYOFFS

DETROIT RED WINGS
THE PLAYOFFS

ROUND 1 — DETROIT vs. NASHVILLE
ROUND 2 — DETROIT vs. COLORADO
ROUND 3 — DETROIT vs. DALLAS
STANLEY CUP — DETROIT vs. PITTSBURGH

GAME 1 – APRIL 10, 2008
One down, 15 to go

 VS.
NASHVILLE 1   **DETROIT 3**

DETROIT -- Henrik Zetterberg scored seven-minutes into the third period to give the Red Wings a 3-1 win and a 1-0 series lead over the Nashville Predators in their best-of-seven Western Conference quarterfinal series.

Detroit entered the 2008 Stanley Cup playoffs with high expectations. The Wings won the Presidents' Trophy for best overall record, after finishing the regular-season with a league-best 53-21-7 record.

"The first one is always very, very difficult," Wings coach Mike Babcock said. "That's what the playoffs are about. Just try not to give up too much and wait for your opportunity."

Dominik Hasek made 19 saves and Johan Franzen scored his fifth career playoff goal to help earn the victory.

"It's always good to get the first goal," Franzen said. "I don't know … play hard in the corners and try to hang onto the puck and get to the net as soon as you can and shot it. It's been bouncing my way." **DR**

THREE STARS

HENRIK ZETTERBERG — DETROIT RED WINGS
JOHAN FRANZEN — DETROIT RED WINGS
DAN ELLIS — NASHVILLE PREDATORS

2007-08 STANLEY CUP CHAMPIONS

DETROIT RED WINGS
THE PLAYOFFS

Opposite Bottom: Johan Franzen lifts a backhand shot past Nashville goalie Dan Ellis during the playoff opener at Joe Louis Arena. (Photo by Tom Turrill/NHLI via Getty Images)

Opposite Top: Franzen reacts advantageously to his first-period goal that gave the Wings a 1-0 lead against the Predators in Game 1 of their Western Conference quarterfinal series. (Photo by Tom Turrill/NHLI via Getty Images)

Tomas Holmstrom, Pavel Datsyuk, Henrik Zetterberg and Chris Chelios celebrate Zetterberg's game-winning goal at 6:54 of the third period of Game 1 against the Predators.

2007-08 STANLEY CUP CHAMPIONS

THE PLAYOFFS

GAME 2 – APRIL 12, 2008

Timeout breathes life into Wings

 vs.

NASHVILLE 2   DETROIT 4

DETROIT -- Mike Babcock called a time-out in the second period to refocus his squad after Nashville scored two goals in 11-seconds to tie the game. Fourteen seconds later, Kris Draper scored his first goal of the postseason, and it was all Detroit from that point on. Tomas Holmstrom finished the scoring and goalie Dominik Hasek made 25 saves in the third to wrap a 4-2 win, giving the Red Wings a 2-0 lead in the best-of-seven series with the Predators.

"All I said was, are we better than this?" Babcock said. "Let's just settle down, play with poise and do our job. We got a smart group, they were doing that with themselves anyways, we thought that it was time to get back on track."

Nicklas Lidstrom scored his first goal of the playoffs and Darren McCarty collected his first NHL goal since April 25, 2006, and Hockeytown went wild when he found the back of the net. DR

THREE STARS

PAVEL DATSYUK
DETROIT RED WINGS

ALEXANDER RADULOV
NASHVILLE PREDATORS

TOMAS HOLMSTROM
DETROIT RED WINGS

2007-08 STANLEY CUP CHAMPIONS

DETROIT RED WINGS
THE PLAYOFFS

Nashville forward Radek Bonk slides into the net with the puck after being checked by Brad Stuart in the first period of Game 2. Despite the Predators' celebration, referees ruled that the puck crossed the line after the net was knocked of its moorings.

Opposite Top: Darren McCarty fired the puck into the open net giving the Red Wings a 1-0 lead in the first period of Game 2. The Wings won, 4-2. (Photo by Tom Turrill/NHLI via Getty Images)

Opposite Bottom: Pavel Datsyuk fires one of his two shots on goal toward Preds goalie Dan Ellis during Game 2. Datsyuk also won 10 of 15 face offs and contributed three hits and two takeaways in the win. (Photo by Tom Turrill/NHLI via Getty Images)

2007-08 STANLEY CUP CHAMPIONS

THE PLAYOFFS

GAME 3 - APRIL 14, 2008

Predators' quick trigger downs Wings

 VS.

NASHVILLE 5   **DETROIT 3**

NASHVILLE – For the second time in the series, the Predators scored a pair of goals seconds apart and took some of the momentum away from the Red Wings.

Jason Arnott scored with 3:58 left in the final period, the second Nashville goal in nine-seconds, and the Predators rallied to beat the Wings, 5-3, cutting their series deficit in half.

"There's moments that are going to happen in a series that can change the whole series," Preds coach Barry Trotz said. "I don't know, we might have just had ours."

Detroit had outshot Nashville in each of the first two games of the series, but the Predators outshot the Wings, 29-26, and scored two more goals than it had in the first two games combined.

"We sure thought we were set up pretty well," Wings coach Mike Babock said. "It looked like things were going real good. It was a good momentum swing for them, and we didn't handle it very good."

THREE STARS

JASON ARNOTT — NASHVILLE PREDATORS
RYAN SUTER — NASHVILLE PREDATORS
DAVID LEGWAND — NASHVILLE PREDATORS

2007-08 STANLEY CUP CHAMPIONS

DETROIT RED WINGS
THE PLAYOFFS

The Nashville fans got into the act as Ryan Suter (20) and Jan Hlavac (17) celebrate David Legwand's second-period goal that tied the score at 2-2. (Photo by John Russell/NHLI via Getty Images)

Opposite Bottom: Jiri Hudler's second-period power-play goal game the Red Wings a 2-0 lead over Nashville on Game 3. Unfortunately, the Predators stormed back with five goals before posting a 5-3 win. (Photo by Chris Graythen/Getty Images)

Opposite Top: Nashville's Ryan Suter celebrates his game-tying goal with David Legwand (11) and J.P. Dumont (71) as Wings goalie Dominik Hasek skates back to the crease in Game 3. (Photo by John Russell/NHLI via Getty Images)

2007-08 STANLEY CUP CHAMPIONS

THE PLAYOFFS

GAME 4 - APRIL 16, 2008

Nashville evens Round 1 series at 2-2

 VS.

NASHVILLE 2   DETROIT 3

NASHVILLE – After Game 4, the league's best team finds itself in a first-round fight.

Dan Hamhuis and Shea Weber scored in 32-second span, and the Predators evened the series against the top-seeded Red Wings with a 3-2 victory.

Dan Ellis stopped 39 shots, Greg de Vries added a goal and Martin Erat had two assists as the eighth-seeded Predators grabbed a lead in the first period and never let up on the Red Wings, even chasing Dominik Hasek from the game in the second.

"We haven't done anything yet," proclaimed Preds coach Barry Trotz. "The only satisfaction is we got a win tonight."

Pavel Datsyuk scored twice for Detroit, and Nashville became the first team to go from trailing to leading in under 10 seconds by scoring two goals within nine seconds.

"The one thing that is really hurting us in this series is, we score a goal and then they get one right away," Wings center Kris Draper said. "When we get momentum, we have to figure out a way to keep it."

THREE STARS

DAN ELLIS — NASHVILLE PREDATORS   SHEA WEBER — NASHVILLE PREDATORS   PAVEL DATSYUK — DETROIT RED WINGS

2007-08 STANLEY CUP CHAMPIONS

DETROIT RED WINGS
THE PLAYOFFS

Opposite Bottom: The Predators celebrate after a goal by Shea Weber gave them a 2-0 lead in the second period of Game 4 at the Sommet Center. (Photo by Chris Graythen/Getty Images)

Opposite Top: Pavel Datsyuk found it difficult to control the puck with Nashville's Jason Arnott playing a tougher brand of hockey in Game 4. (Photo by Chris Graythen/Getty Images)

Chris Osgood stops a shot by J.P. Dumont. Osgood, who entered the game in the second period in relief of Dominik Hasek, stopped all 13 shots that he faced. (Photo by John Russell/NHLI via Getty Images)

2007-08 STANLEY CUP CHAMPIONS

THE PLAYOFFS

GAME 5 - APRIL 18, 2008

Wings regain series lead; ride Mule to overtime win

NASHVILLE 1 VS. DETROIT 2

DETROIT — As quickly as Nashville had tied it late, Detroit resurrected the Joe Louis Arena crowd from silent shock into absolute euphoria.

Nashville's JP Dumont passed right to Red Wings' Niklas Kronwall, who sent Johan Franzen in on a breakaway. The Wings' right wing deked left to right before squeezing the overtime game-winner between Dan Ellis and the left post.

With the 2-1 overtime win, Detroit took a 3-2 series lead back to Nashville, the site of Game 6 on Sunday.

"You're determined," Wings captain Nicklas Lidstrom said. "You want to make the right play. You're not going to throw it away. We showed that as a team, too. We weren't going to be denied."

For 54 minutes in regulation, the Wings clung to a 1-0 lead. They badly out-shot and out-chanced the Predators.

But Detroit couldn't beat Ellis a second time, and with the seconds ticking down in regulation, Radek Bonk found the puck in a crowd and sent the game to overtime.

Chris Osgood started his first playoff game since 2001, and made 20 saves.

THREE STARS

JOHAN FRANZEN — DETROIT RED WINGS
CHRIS OSGOOD — DETROIT RED WINGS
DAN ELLIS — NASHVILLE PREDATORS

2007-08 STANLEY CUP CHAMPIONS

Opposite Top: Game 5 was a physical affair as was evident in Dan Cleary's hit on Nashville's Ryan Suter.

Opposite Bottom: Looks like a double-standard as Nashville goalie Dan Ellis picks up and tosses an octopus off the ice during Game 5.

Johan Franzen scored another game-winner, but this one was the decisive goal in the Game 5 overtime win at Joe Louis Arena.

DETROIT RED WINGS
THE PLAYOFFS

ROUND 1 — DETROIT vs. NASHVILLE

GAME 6 - APRIL 20, 2008

Lucky bounce clinches it

 vs.

NASHVILLE 0   **DETROIT 3**

NASHVILLE – A talented Red Wings' squad got pretty lucky in Game 6.

Nicklas Lidstrom bounced in a short-handed goal over Dan Ellis from beyond center ice and the Red Wings closed out the Predators with 3-0 win.

"I'm just trying to float one in there," said Lidstrom of his second-period goal that gave the Wings a 1-0 lead. "I took some off the shot just to see if I could land in front of him, just go for a bounce or just create something in front of him."

Jiri Hudler added a goal in the third with Brian Rafalski adding an empty-netter with 4.8 seconds left. Goalie Chris Osgood stopped 20 shots for the shutout in his second straight playoff start as top-seeded Detroit became the first road team to win in this series.

With the victory, Detroit also passed Toronto for second on the list of playoff series won with 59.

"Anytime you get the opportunity to close out an opponent you want to do it as quick as you can," Wings center Kris Draper said. **DR**

THREE STARS

NICKLAS LIDSTROM — DETROIT RED WINGS
DAN ELLIS — NASHVILLE PREDATORS
DAVID LEGWAND — NASHVILLE PREDATORS

ROUND 2 — DETROIT vs. COLORADO
ROUND 3 — DETROIT vs. DALLAS
STANLEY CUP — DETROIT vs. PITTSBURGH

2007-08 STANLEY CUP CHAMPIONS

DETROIT RED WINGS
THE PLAYOFFS

Chris Osgood eyes the puck while Brian Rafalski makes sure that Dan Hamhuis (2) can't get a scoring chance. (Photo by John Russell/NHLI via Getty Images)

Opposite Top: Nicklas Lidstrom is congratulated by a happy Red Wings' bench after his short-handed goal from beyond center ice skipped by Nashville goalie Dan Ellis. In Game 6. (Photo by John Russell/NHLI via Getty Images)

Opposite Bottom: Chris Osgood, who relived Dominik Hasek in Game 4, shares some thoughts with his Nashville counterpart, Dan Ellis, after the Wings clinched the series with a 3-0 win in Game 6 at the Sommet Center. (Photo by John Russell/NHLI via Getty Images)

2007-08 STANLEY CUP CHAMPIONS

MAY 24, 2008

Tentacle Tradition

By Michael Caples

Nothing quite says Red Wings hockey like an octopus.

The slimy, eight-tentacled creature has been the symbol for the Red Wings playoffs since the first one found its way to the ice in 1952. Ever since, Hockeytown can't get enough of the octopi tradition.

Standing in the midst of octopi fever is Kevin Dean, co-owner of Superior Fish Company in Royal Oak, Mich. When the Red Wings began to rebuild their dynasty in the early 1990s, Dean jumped at the opportunity to rebuild a lost tradition.

Today, Superior Fish, in suburban Detroit, is the "O-Fish-Al" octopi store. The 'Al' part is in honor of Al Sobotka, the famed Zamboni driver and octopus twirler at Joe Louis Arena.

Signs featuring the slogan and a smiling octopus welcome you into a store adorned with Red Wings jerseys, sticks and memorabilia. A glass display case located next to the main counter features a 20-pound version of the Wings' unofficial mascot, its tentacles outstretched to show its massive size.

Dean says that during the playoffs, the store goes from being known as "the house of quality" to "the house of octopi". And game days are when Dean and his brother, David, have Superior Fish focused on the Wings' success.

On playoff game days, octopi sales increase from an average of three per day to 25. During the 1998 Stanley Cup finals, Dean said they sold over 100 octopi a day.

"We'll have our octopus display set up, which is like a religious icon," Dean said. "We have gained a reputation so a lot of people come with their kids to see the giant octopus display.

"If there's home games, we'll have some Red Wings' fans come in, especially right around closing time as they make their way down to 'The Joe' to pick up an octopus for whatever purposes they desire."

Dean provides those who purchase octopi with a pamphlet that gives information for two options – consumption or propulsion. The 'Octoquette' section gives guidelines for the proper decorum if one chooses to propel an octopus.

Top: A Red Wings' fan throws an octopus over the glass during Game 1 of the Western Conference semifinal against Colorado. Tossing octopi on the ice at Joe Louis Arena has been a tradition that dates back to 1952 at Olympia Stadium.

Above: Linesmen Jean Morin and Scott Driscoll had the dirty job of shoveling an octopus from the ice before the start of Game 1 against the Avalanche.

CAN'T MAKE A GAME?

Simply forward or sell your tickets to someone who can.

My Red Wings Account is your one-stop location for forwarding tickets to family, friends, or clients via e-mail, paying your invoices online, and updating your account profile. You can also post your tickets for sale so that other fans can enjoy the game when you can't.

Make the most of your season ticket investment.

Visit detroitredwings.com

provided by ticketmaster

"We always make sure they see the octoquette," Dean said. "That is especially for the tad amount of people who plan on taking theirs to 'The Joe'."

Dean said the new NHL rules limiting Sobotka's famed octopus swings are putting a damper on a great sports tradition. During the first round, NHL officials declared that Sobotka would be fined if he picked an octopus off the ice and swung it on the ice.

"It is a great hockey tradition, some people don't like traditions," Dean said.

The hockey tradition has also led to a higher consumption of octopus in metro Detroit, which Dean says is a great source of protein with little fat. Octopus is known as the 'hot dog' of the world. Before the tradition re-emerged, octopi was primarily eaten at Greek and Italian restaurants, but the public interest grew with the Red Wings' success, according to Dean.

"It raised the awareness of our building and our company," he said, "but also it has raised the awareness of the octopus as a food source. Just like the pumpkin's put out during Halloween on the doorstep, but also people are making pumpkin pie, eating the pumpkin seeds, the same thing with the octopus."

The tradition and the Royal Oak store have drawn national attention from cable networks like ESPN and CNN. The store has even been featured on a Japanese game show, all types of Swedish media, even the front page of the Washington Post. However, Dean's favorite media coverage came in the form of "Hockey Night in Canada" and hockey icon Don Cherry.

HNIC visited Superior Fish in 1997 as Cherry and Ron MacLean filmed a spot about the tradition. Cherry stood behind the counter with Dean, selling octopi and talking about the Red Wings.

Dean said that the best part, however, was what Cherry did to help the business. After filming, Cherry and McLean went to the back of the store for interviews with local media, and Cherry made sure Superior Fish was mentioned.

When the Red Wings reach the Cup finals, Dean said that's the time when the Superior Fish team rises to the next level.

"When we go to the finals, as we have been going for a good percentage, we will have an octopus taste-fest," Dean said. "We'll have octopus chili, barbequed octopus, octopus salad and some different smoked octopus dips for people to come here so they can savor the flavor of a hockey tradition."

The eight tentacles may not accurately represent the playoffs anymore, but there's no mistake that the octopi tradition is a Red Wings' tradition. And Superior Fish plans to keep their end of the bargain for years to come. **DR**

Above Left: Kevin Dean prepares an eight-tentacled creature from its inky abyss.

Left: A big supporter of the octopi tradition and of Al Sobotka is hockey icon Don Cherry.

Above: Al Sobotka revs up the fans before Game 1 Western Conference quarterfinal against Nashville at Joe Louis Arena.

THE PLAYOFFS

GAME 1 - APRIL 4, 2008

Wings dominate Avs, chase Theodore in Game 1

 VS.

COLORADO 3   DETROIT 4

DETROIT — Without Peter Forsberg and several other injured players missing from the Avalanche's lineup, much of the pre-series hype was missing before Game 1.

While some of the nostalgia of past playoff series was missing, the Red Wings held on, taking Game 1 of the Western Conference semifinal in nail-biting fashion, 4-3.

Johan had two goals and an assist, Dan Cleary scored his first goal of the playoffs, and Henrik Zetterberg also scored in the victory.

"It's gonna be a talented, free-flowing series but it's gonna be in the trenches, too," Wings goalie Chris Osgood said. "Behind the net. In front. And we gotta keep our composure. I thought we did a great job. There's going to be momentum swings that are going to be huge in this series and go back and forth."

Once Franzen put the Wings up 4-1, Avs coach Joel Quenneville had seen enough of goalie Jose Theodore, who was yanked in favor Peter Budaj.

"Jose was sick last night," Quenneville said. "Normally, he skates the morning of a game. But he rested all day and he wanted to play. He's not feeling great. But hopefully, it's a short spell and he'll be fine."

Four minutes after the goaltender change, Colorado started its comeback bid with goals by John-Michael Liles and Milan Hejduk.

THREE STARS

JOHAN FRANZEN - DETROIT RED WINGS
PAUL STASTNY - COLORADO AVALANCHE
HENRIK ZETTERBERG - DETROIT RED WINGS

2007-08 STANLEY CUP CHAMPIONS

DETROIT RED WINGS
THE PLAYOFFS

Opposite Top: Linesman Scott Driscoll was all smiles while on octopi duty prior to the Red Wings' Game 1 encounter with the Colorado Avalanche.

Opposite Bottom: Tomas Holmstrom and the rest of the Wings provided a limited view for Avs goalie Jose Theodore, who eventually was removed in the first two games at Joe Louis Arena.

The scoreboard doesn't show it, but Johan Franzen's second goal, gave the Wings a 4-1 lead early in the second period. Moments later, Theodore headed to the bench in favor of back-up goalie Peter Budaj.

2007-08 STANLEY CUP CHAMPIONS

THE PLAYOFFS

GAME 2 – APRIL 26, 2008

Mule's trick sends Theodore packing again

 VS.

COLORADO 1   DETROIT 5

DETROIT -- Johan Franzen earned his first career hat trick, the Red Wings chased the opposing goalie for the second straight game, and Darren McCarty sent the Joe Louis Arena crowd into an uproar with a second-period fight Saturday.

The outcome was perhaps the Wings' best post-season performance of these playoffs, as they out-played, out-hustled and out-shot the Colorado Avalanche in Game 2 of the best-of-seven Western Conference semifinal series.

Detroit scored three goals in the second period and Chris Osgood made 19 saves, en route to an impressive 5-1 victory.

Franzen's playoff hat trick is the first since 2002, when McCarty scored three in a 5-3 win over Colorado in the Western Conference final.

"He was playing real well the last month and a half and he's playing real well now, making the most of his opportunity," Wings coach Mike Babcock said. "He's a big man with a lot of skill and good hands. When you can't get the puck off the guy and he gets in tight, he's tough for the goalie to handle."

Valtteri Filppula and Henrik Zetterberg also scored and Niklas Kronwall added a pair of assists for Detroit. Ian Laperriere scored the Avs' lone goal.

"Whatever it is, everybody should get a piece of that," said Nicklas Lidstrom of Franzen. "It's great to see him take the puck to the net. He really tries to hang on to it. He's scoring goals where he's just being patient and going to the front of the net. We wanted to try and hang on to the puck down low and make their whole five-man unit play defense. We've been successful at doing that."

THREE STARS

JOHAN FRANZEN — NIKLAS KRONWAL — HENRIK ZETTERBERG

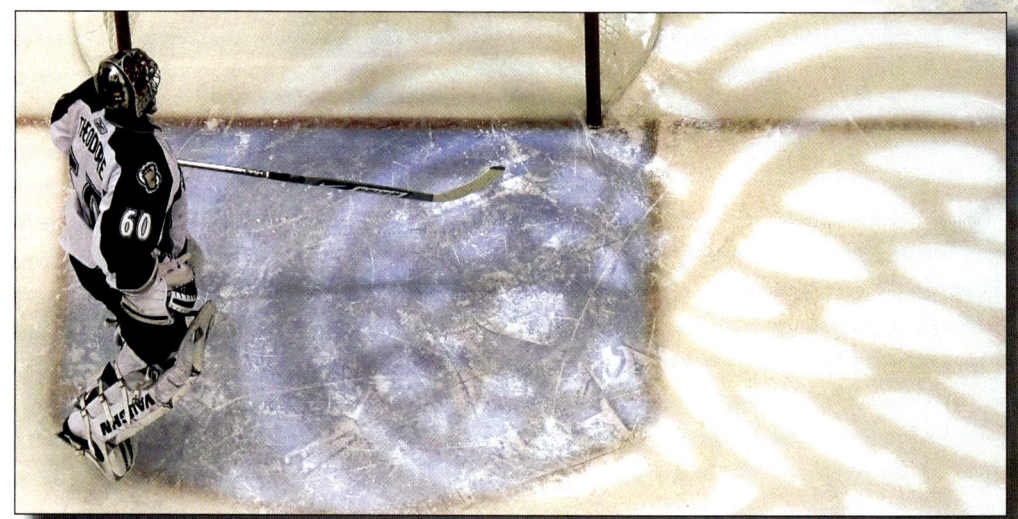

DETROIT RED WINGS
THE PLAYOFFS

Franzen tipped in a shot from the point on the power play, giving the Wings a 1-0 lead in the first. He scored two more times, giving him his first career hat trick.

Opposite Bottom: Avs goalie Jose Theodore is awash in a Red Wings' light show. A short time later the veteran surrendered four goals on 20 shots in just over half the game. He was pulled after Zetterberg's goal made it 4-0. (Photo by Gregory Shamus/Getty Images)

Opposite Top: The Wings played a solid style of lockdown defense on Avs forward Ryan Smyth, and limiting Colorado to 20 shots on goal and holding them to 0-for-5 on the power play.

2007-08 STANLEY CUP CHAMPIONS

THE PLAYOFFS

GAME 3 – APRIL 29, 2008

Wings put stranglehold on Avalanche

COLORADO 3 vs. **DETROIT 4**

DENVER -- For the first time in the series, the Red Wings didn't score first. But it wasn't long before Detroit built a 3-1 lead en route to its third straight win over a hapless Colorado Avalanche squad that seemed to have more bodies in the trainer's room than on the ice.

Pavel Datsyuk scored twice and Johan Franzen continued his torrid pace, collecting his sixth goal of the series, putting the Red Wings on the verge of advancing to the Western Conference finals for the second straight season with a 4-3 win Tuesday at the Pepsi Center.

"There were no defensemen on either goal," Datsyuk told the Associated Press. "All I had to worry about was the goalie."

Though center Peter Forsberg and defenseman Scott Hannan returned to the Avs lineup, their worries were plentiful with injuries still sidelining forward Ryan Smyth (foot), and that was before Paul Stastny, their leading scorer, went down in the first period.

Colorado was also without forward Wojtek Wolski (shoulder) for the series. Forsberg (groin) missed both games in Detroit and Hannan missed Game 2 with a lower-body injury.

The Red Wings can wrap up the series with a win in Game 4 on Thursday at the Pepsi Center. None of the five previous playoff series between the rivals ended in a sweep.

The Red Wings took a 4-2 lead into the third period, and goalie Chris Osgood, who made 30 saves, made sure the lead held up.

"Our power play was good and we played great 5-on-5," Osgood told the AP. "We put pucks on the net and created goals. We took too many penalties to let them back in the game and gave them some momentum at the end. But we held on at the end."

THREE STARS

PAVEL DATSYUK
DETROIT RED WINGS

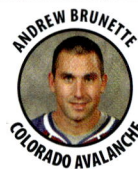
ANDREW BRUNETTE
COLORADO AVALANCHE

HENRIK ZETTERBERG
DETROIT RED WINGS

2007-08 STANLEY CUP CHAMPIONS

DETROIT RED WINGS
THE PLAYOFFS

Datsyuk is congratulated by teammates after scoring in the first period in Game 3. The Wings won, 4-3, to take a 3-0 series lead over Colorado in the Western Conference semifinal. (Photo by Doug Pensinger/Getty Images)

Opposite Top: Chris Osgood makes one of his 30 saves in Game 3. (Photo by Michael Martin/NHLI via Getty Images)

Opposite Below: Datsyuk did in the Avs with two goals in Game 3. Here he controls the puck as Colorado defenseman John-Michael Liles tries to slow down the Wings' forward. (Photo by Doug Pensinger/Getty Images)

2007-08 STANLEY CUP CHAMPIONS

DETROIT RED WINGS
THE PLAYOFFS

GAME 4 - MAY 1, 2008

Wings crush Colorado, advance to conference finals

COLORADO 2   **DETROIT 8**

DENVER -- This certainly wasn't expected.

Yet while nobody anticipated that the Red Wings would sweep the Colorado Avalanche or beat them badly, 8-2, in the series clincher Thursday, it does come with a nice gift -- a pleasant break before Detroit plays for the Western Conference championship.

"I won't apologize for beating them like this," Henrik Zetterberg told the Associated Press. "I know they'll come back at us next year."

Johan Franzen continued his torrid playoff pace while passing aside more of Gordie Howe's franchise records.

In March, Franzen's six game-winning goals passed Mr. Hockey's original mark of five in a month set in February 1952, and on Thursday, the Mule scored three goals in the Red Wings' blowout victory, giving him nine in the four-game sweep. Howe's record of eight goals in a series had stood since 1949.

"He's been great. He's a big, big man with lots of skill. We're lucky to have him," Wings coach Mike Babcock told AP. "We feel good about that. I'm not taking anything away from what we did, but their team was depleted by the end here.

"He's been big now for a long time. He broke Gordie's record in March, and then he broke his record here today. So good for him. If you're going to break records, you might as well break Gordie Howe's."

For Franzen Thursday's hat trick was his second in three games against the Avs. His nine goals in the series matched Colorado's total. He is the first player with two hat tricks in one series since Jari Kurri did it for Edmonton in 1985.

The Mule scored on a breakaway in the first period and added a short-handed tally and a redirection into the net in the second, when the Red Wings scored four times to build a 7-1 edge.

"I think they gave up after 4-1," Franzen said, "so I got a couple of freebies."

Franzen had a hat trick in Game 2, and is only the second player in team history to post two hat tricks in one playoff series, joining Norm Ullman, who did it against Chicago in 1964.

THREE STARS

JOHAN FRANZEN — DETROIT RED WINGS   HENRIK ZETTERBERG — DETROIT RED WINGS   MIKAEL SAMUELSSON — DETROIT RED WINGS

2007-08 STANLEY CUP CHAMPIONS

DETROIT RED WINGS
THE PLAYOFFS

The hits kept coming for Wings defenseman Niklas Kronwall, who draws contact with former Michigan star T.J. Hensick during Game 4. Kronwall set a tone through the playoffs with a physical style. (Photo by Doug Pensinger/Getty Images)

Oppostie Below: Colorado captain Joe Sakic congratulates Johan Franzen after the Wings swept the Avs from the playoffs. Franzen had a hat trick in Game 4 and finished the series with nine goals, including a three-goal performance in Game 2. (Photo by Doug Pensinger/Getty Images)

Opposite Top: Pavel Datsyuk celebrates one of Henrik Zetterberg's two second-period goals in Game 4. The Wings scored four times in the period – two power-play and one short-handed – in building a 7-1 lead. (Photo by Michael Martin/NHLI via Getty Images)

2007-08 STANLEY CUP CHAMPIONS

MAY 6, 2008

Father Fan

By Lindsey Ungar

CANTON, Mich. — On a Saturday in April one of Detroit's biggest Red Wings' fans faced a real dilemma.

It was late in the afternoon and the Red Wings were set to host Colorado in Game 2 of the Western Conference semifinal. Father Patrick Casey had tickets — bought in advance — to the game at Joe Louis Arena. But he also had three other commitments – presiding over a wedding, hearing confessions and celebrating Mass.

Fr. Casey, pastor of St. Thomas a'Becket Catholic Church, couldn't make it downtown. But this diehard Wings' fan still managed to catch the game — sort of.

"So I'm hearing confessions, and I rush (into my office) and turn on the radio, and oh, it's 1-0," Casey said.

Before Mass began, he listened to the Wings go up 4-0 on the Avalanche. During his homily, he talked about obedience to the Lord, whom the parishioners should love above all things. But he didn't ignore his love for the Wings, asking those in attendance, "Who here is a Red Wings' fan?"

From the back of church, a voice booms, 'It's 5-1!'

Casey, a native of Waterford Township, Mich., says there's a fine line between religion and his favorite hometown team. He's never prayed for a Wings' victory. He doesn't don jerseys around the Parish — just a pair of Red Wings cufflinks. And he won't honor requests to wear his infamous Red Wings vestment at weddings, either.

"I tread this fine line because it's the eternal realities that I'm supposed to be drawing people to, not staying in the mundane things of this earth," Casey said. "So it's a fine line. But you still gotta connect to people's experiences.

"It's not all about sports, but sports are always a great analogy. In Paul's Letter to Timothy, (he wrote) 'I fought the good fight, I have finished the race.' St. Paul uses all these athletic images. So you try and use things that people can hunker down to."

Casey first got noticed for his fandom back in 2002. At the time, Casey was pastor at St. Dominic on Detroit's west side. One of his parishioners, who had made vestments for him in the past, asked him to lead a pilgrimage to Medjugorje, Bosnia-Herzegovina. His response?

"I just kind of flippantly said, 'Well yeah, I'll lead a group if you make this vestment for me.' She was not happy about it because she's very conservative. But she decided going to Medjugorje was more important than the vestment so she made the vestment for me. She just told me, 'Don't tell anyone where you got it from.'"

Newspapers across the country ran a photo of him at Mass draped in the cream-colored vestment painted with a Red Wings' logo. Detroit went on to hoist its 10th Stanley Cup that spring.

That same vestment is now draped over the statue of St. Thomas a'Becket at his current parish, where he became pastor in 2004.

But Casey isn't the only Wingnut in his congregation. Joan Kijek, Cathy Piasta and Anne Truax, who work in the religious education department, are known as the Grind Line.

"Because we do all the hard work," Kijek joked.

Kijek always wears red on game days, and switches to jerseys for playoff games. She drives a red van with a huge Wings' logo on the back window. She also named her dog, Ozzie, as a tribute to Wings goalie Chris Osgood. And during the playoffs, the picture that hangs outside her office no longer shows the holy family — it's swapped for a panorama of Joe Louis Arena, with her name glowing on the Jumbotron.

But it doesn't look out of place in a church office decked with Red Wings posters, clippings, and yes, even a Wingnuts hat.

"The day I came to meet the staff, probably half of them all had Red Wings jerseys on," Casey said. "I felt very much at home when I got here."

Casey never played hockey, but he fell in love with the Wings while attending Sacred Heart Major Seminary in Detroit, and became a full-fledged citizen of Hockeytown when he was ordained in 1997 — the year the Wings snapped a 42-year Stanley Cup drought. He attended a dozen games that season, many at the thanks of area funeral directors, which are constantly vying for his business.

Although he missed most of Game 2 against Colorado, he didn't miss Game 3. And as he watched, Casey had just one thought, one shared by many Red Wings' fans this postseason: "I saw a team going all the way to the Stanley Cup this year."

congrats to the Detroit Red Wings

for bringing the championship back to

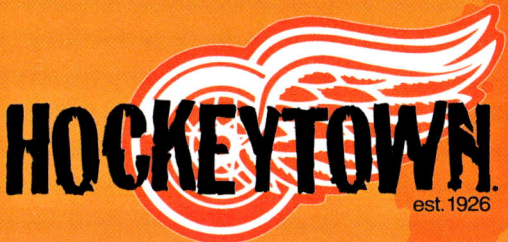

 Stay connected to your Detroit Red Wings with Advanced TV, wireless service, and high-speed Internet all from the new AT&T.

The new

THE PLAYOFFS

GAME 1 - MAY 8, 2008

Wings make Turco see red; Grab 1-0 series lead

 VS.

DALLAS 1   DETROIT 4

DETROIT — For seemingly the entire game, Dallas goalie Marty Turco was seeing red.

Tomas Holmstrom. Johan Franzen. Holmstrom again. Crowding the crease on the power play, the Red Wings prevented Turco from seeing the puck until it was too late.

"Every game it's tough to see all the shots," Turco said. "We've done a great job blocking them and dictating the play of where we want it to come from and that just wasn't the case tonight."

And Turco still hasn't seen his team win in Detroit, as the Red Wings won Thursday's Western Conference finals opener, 4-1, of their best-of-seven series.

Franzen and Holmstrom each collected a goal, and defensemen Nicklas Lidstrom and Niklas Kronwall each had two assists in the win. Brian Rafalski and Valtteri Filppula also scored for Detroit.

With Mattias Norstrom already whistled for hooking, Mark Fistric and Holmstrom mixed it up in front of Turco. Only Fistric was nailed with a penalty, putting the Red Wings in a 5-on-3 situation just over four minutes into the contest.

Lidstrom's point shot rung off the goalpost, but Rafalski potted the long rebound from the slot, putting the Red Wings up 1-0.

It was Franzen's turn on Detroit's second tally — again with the man-advantage — late in the first period. Kronwall's point shot, Franzen deflected through Turco's legs.

Turco was again looking behind him to the find the puck on the third Wings' power-play goal. Holmstrom, almost resting atop Turco's butterfly, deflected Lidstrom's snapshot past the Dallas netminder.

Chris Osgood stopped 20 of 21 shots faced, winning his seventh straight start.

THREE STARS

TOMAS HOLMSTROM   NICKLAS LIDSTROM   NIKLAS KRONWALL
DETROIT RED WINGS   DETROIT RED WINGS   DETROIT RED WINGS

2007-08 STANLEY CUP CHAMPIONS

DETROIT RED WINGS
THE PLAYOFFS

Opposite Top: Red Wings like Tomas Holmstrom made life miserable for Dallas goalie Marty Turco in Game 1. Holmstrom and Johan Franzen set up shop in front and the Stars' crease all night and each collected a power-play goal.

Opposite Bottom: Even when he did have help from his defensemen, Turco had a difficult time containing Franzen in front of the net.

Meanwhile, on the other side of the rink, Chris Osgood had plenty of help from the unselfish play of guys like Kris Draper, who had one of the Wings' 12 blocks in Game 1.

2007-08 STANLEY CUP CHAMPIONS

THE PLAYOFFS

DALLAS 1   DETROIT 2

GAME 2 - MAY 10, 2008

Even without Mule, Wings dig hole for Stars

DETROIT — Prior to Game 2, Detroit faced the reality that its leading scorer, Johan Franzen, would miss the game with concussion-like symptoms.

But even without the Mule, Dallas goalie Marty Turco's focus was still on the six-feet of blue paint in front of him.

With Dallas defenseman Mattias Norstrom and Turco tag-teaming Tomas Holmstrom on a late first-period power play, Henrik Zetterberg's point shot deflected off Mike Modano's stick past Turco. That built a 2-1 lead for the Red Wings, which they never relinquished to take a 2-0 lead in the Western Conference finals.

The Red Wings have scored 10 power-play goals in their last five games.

Playing just over two minutes in the first period, Darren Helm opened up the scoring, rushing down the left side, he found the top shelf past Turco's glove.

"(Jiri) Hudler made a great play and I was able to put it in," said Helm who scored his first NHL goal. "I was glad to contribute on the score for the team tonight."

After Chris Osgood, who stopped 17 shots, bumped into Brenden Morrow, Stephane Robidas sent a one-timed slapshot from the point past the Detroit netminder to tie the game.

Osgood faced more scoring chances Saturday than in Game 1. Early in the third period, he preserved the Wings' one-goal lead with a last-ditch effort. Sliding away from the play, Osgood kicked out his left pad to get a piece of Modano's wrist shot.

THREE STARS

HENRIK ZETTERBERG — DETROIT RED WINGS   VALTTERI FILPPULA — DETROIT RED WINGS   DARREN HELM — DETROIT RED WINGS

2007-08 STANLEY CUP CHAMPIONS

DETROIT RED WINGS
THE PLAYOFFS

Opposing Top: The Red Wings were a happy bunch when they took a 2-1 lead on the Stars in Game 2 on Henrik Zetterberg's first-period goal at Joe Louis Arena.

Opposing Below: Goalie Chris Osgood peers over at teammate Brett Lebda was injured – albeit momentarily – during Game 2.

Kris Draper restrains Mike Ribeiro after the Stars' center slashed goalie Chris Osgood at the end of Game 2 of the Western Conference finals. The Red Wings defeated the Stars 2-1. (Photo by Dave Sandford/Getty Images)

2007-08 STANLEY CUP CHAMPIONS

THE PLAYOFFS

GAME 3 - MAY 12, 2008

Datsyuk's hat trick lifts Red Wings to 3-0 series edge

DALLAS 2 VS. DETROIT 5

DALLAS — The Euro Twins struck when it counted most for the Red Wings when the Western Conference finals shifted to Dallas for Game 3.

Up a goal in the third period, Henrik Zetterberg scored a short-handed goal and Pavel Datsyuk added the clincher with his third goal of the game en route to the Wings' 5-2 victory Monday night. For Datsyuk the three-goal performance was his first career hat trick.

Zetterberg added two assists sending Detroit to a 3-0 series lead over the Stars.

The win was the Red Wings' ninth straight playoff victory, the best streak in a single playoff season in franchise history.

"There's a lot of experience in here," center Kris Draper told the Associated Press. "We're not getting caught up in the little things. We have a chance to eliminate a great hockey team."

Detroit came out focused on the scoreboard than settling a score with Mike Ribeiro for his slash on goalie Chris Osgood at the end of Game 2. Both players were fined, but not suspended by the league.

The early energy came from Dallas being home for the first time since a four-overtime win over San Jose that ended the previous round. The Stars responded with strong play early, but couldn't get the puck past Osgood. Then Datsyuk beat goalie Marty Turco midway through the first. Datsyuk struck again later in the period, just 37 seconds after the Stars tied it at 1-1.

THREE STARS

PAVEL DATSYUK
DETROIT RED WINGS

HENRIK ZETTERBERG
DETROIT RED WINGS

BRIAN RAFALSKI
DETROIT RED WINGS

2007-08 STANLEY CUP CHAMPIONS

Opposite Top: Pavel Datsyuk gives the Red Wings a 2-1 lead with this first-period goal beating goalie Marty Turco behind his legs. Datsyuk's hat trick was pivotal in the Wings' 5-2 win. (Photo by Christian Petersen/Getty Images)

Opposite Below: Brad Stuart and Valtteri Filppula helped the Wings limit the Stars' stars, like Mike Ribeiro, from getting quality scoring chances. (Photo by Glenn James/NHLI via Getty Images)

Darren McCarty and Darren Helm help Jiri Hudler celebrate his third goal of the playoffs. Hudler's goal gave the Wings a 3-2 lead in the second period. (Photo by Ronald Martinez/Getty Images)

THE PLAYOFFS

DALLAS 3 VS. **DETROIT 1**

GAME 4 - MAY 14, 2008

Stars get momentum, series life after Wings get goal waved off

DALLAS — Pavel Datsyuk's second-period power-play goal didn't last long, nor did the Wings' momentum in the series after a referee ruled that Tomas Holmstrom interfered with Dallas goalie Marty Turco.

The chain of events seemingly shifted momentum in the favor of the Stars, who kept their playoff chances alive with a 3-1 win on Wednesday, preventing a Red Wings' series sweep.

Loui Ericksson's goal about 12 minutes after Datsyuk's was waved off, then third-period goals from Mike Modano and Brenden Morrow sent the series back to Detroit for Game 5.

"It was a pretty intense, desperate game from everyone on our side," Turco said. "We'll have to continue like that just to have a chance."

Turco made 34 saves.

The loss was Detroit's first since dropping Game 4 to Nashville in the quarterfinals, thus snapping a franchise best nine-game postseason winning streak. As for goalie Chris Osgood, the loss ended a 9-0 run, giving up one goal less than he had in the previous three games combined.

Still, the frustrating events of the second period were on the minds of many in the Red Wings' locker room.

"It's a reputation call, totally. It's disappointing," Wings coach Mike Babcock said.

Had Datsyuk's goal counted, the Wings would've had a 1-0 lead. But the game remained tied until Ericksson scored with less than 30-seconds left in the period, giving the Stars their first lead of the entire series.

Just 49 seconds into the third period, Henrik Zetterberg ripped a shot past Turco, tying the game at 1-1. Still Turco turned aside 14 shots in the second, and 15 more in the third, including a last-minute barrage of 6-on-4 and 6-on-3.

THREE STARS
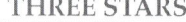

MARTY TURCO — DALLAS STARS
BRENDEN MORROW — DALLAS STARS
MIKE MODANO — DALLAS STARS

DETROIT RED WINGS
THE PLAYOFFS

Loui Eriksson tips the Game 4 tide in the Stars' favor with this second-period goal. (Photo by Christian Petersen/Getty Images)

Bottom: Even in enemy territory, this fan shows his support for the Red Wings during Game 4 of the Western Conference finals at American Airlines Center. (Photo by Christian Petersen/Getty Images)

Opposite Top: For much of Game 4, stopping the puck was as easy as catching pop ups for Marty Turco, who made 34 stops. It was also the first time that the Wings were held to one goal in a game since March 30. (Photo by Christian Petersen/Getty Images)

Opposite Bottom: Nicklas Lidstrom gets an explanation why Pavel Datsyuk's second-period goal didn't count from referee Kelly Sutherland. (Photo by Ronald Martinez/Getty Images)

2007-08 STANLEY CUP CHAMPIONS

THE PLAYOFFS

DALLAS 2   **DETROIT 1**

GAME 5 - MAY 17, 2008

Tailspin sends Wings to second straight loss to Stars

DETROIT — After rattling off a team-record nine straight wins, Detroit failed to close out its Western Conference final series with Dallas for the second straight game, losing 2-1 at Joe Louis Arena on Saturday.

The Stars trail in the best-of-seven series, 3-2, with Game 6 coming Monday in Dallas.

"We were backing up a little bit too much," Nicklas Lidstrom said. "That's giving them room to make plays, and find guys jumping up in the play, too, so you have to tighten up a little bit defensively."

It was the first time the Red Wings have lost in eight home games this postseason and marks the first career victory -- in 12 tries -- for Stars goalie Marty Turco in Detroit.

"Every time he's been backed up against the wall, he's responded," Dallas center Steve Ott said. "He's done that all season."

Dallas is trying to become the first team since the 1975 Islanders to rally from a 3-0 series deficit. That stat is being echoed in the Eastern finals, where Philadelphia kept its Cup hopes alive with a win over Pittsburgh in Game 4.

"There's pressure on both teams," Lidstrom said. "If they lose one game, the series is over. If we win, it's over, too. I don't really feel that pressure. The thing is you have to be ready to play the game that's coming up."

Besides stopping 38 shots, Turco led the breakout on both Dallas goals. His patented stretch passes caught Detroit on two bad line changes.

With Brad Stuart and Lidstrom trying to get off the ice midway through the first, Brett Lebda scrambled to get back in the play. Turco's 80-footer sprung the rush up ice, and Trevor Daley finished it off with his first playoff marker.

"We gave up too many odd-man rushes tonight, for one reason or another," said Wings goalie Chris Osgood, who stopped 19 shots. "That was the most that I've seen in a long time. For one reason or another, they're getting some speed through the neutral zone and getting some guys home-free a couple times. ... Those are the things that bite you."

Jiri Hudler had Detroit's only goal. His power-play tally tied the game at one at 15:30 of the first period, and snapped an 0-for-13 power play slump.

THREE STARS

MARTY TURCO — DALLAS STARS   **JIRI HUDLER** — DETROIT RED WINGS   **JOEL LUNDQVIST** — DALLAS STARS

2007-08 STANLEY CUP CHAMPIONS

DETROIT RED WINGS
THE PLAYOFFS

Dallas Drake made his presence felt in Game 5, delivering this bone-crushing check to Toby Petersen. It was one of three big hits delivered by Drake in one first-period shift. During his sequence, Drake also drilled Stephane Robidas and Petersen a second time. (Photo by Dave Sandford/Getty Images)

Oppostie Top: A linesman has to restrain Stars forward Niklas Hagman and Tomas Holmstrom late in the third period of Game 5.

Opposite Bottom: Marty Turco is congratulated by defensemen Trevor Daley (6) and Mattias Norstrom following the Stars' 2-1 victory in Game 5 at Joe Louis Arena. It was Turco's first win in Detroit since turning pro.

2007-08 STANLEY CUP CHAMPIONS

THE PLAYOFFS

GAME 6 - MAY 19, 2008

Hockeytown returns to Cup finals

DALLAS 1 **DETROIT 4**

DETROIT — Finally, the Red Wings put away the pesky Dallas Stars. Finally, the Red Wings are back in the Stanley Cup finals for the first time since winning it in 2002.

The team that breezed through the regular-season and allowed the fewest goals of any team, rebounded against the Stars, with a 4-1 series-clinching win at American Airlines Center.

Game 6 was the Wings' from the start, as they delivered a series knockout punch to the Stars with a 3-0 first-period lead on goals by Kris Draper, Pavel Datsyuk and Dallas Drake.

"You need everybody to contribute for you to be successful," Wings coach Mike Babcock said. "I thought we really got that tonight. I thought Draper's goal was a great example for everyone; driving the net, knocking your teeth out, score off your lips. To me, those are team things."

Draper's first goal of the series was redirected into the net off his face. With the puck in the net, Draper immediately skated to the bench. After receiving six stitches to his chin, he returned to the game.

For the Red Wings, this is the 23rd time that they have reached the Stanley Cup finals, but first since 2002. Detroit lost to Anaheim in last season's Western Conference finals.

Detroit had the most points in the league this season winning the Presidents' Trophy, which gives them home-ice throughout the playoffs. They have been playing much better for most of the last month and a half, even winning nine straight playoff games in one stretch.

But Dallas, who eliminated Anaheim and San Jose in the first two rounds, bounced back by beating the Wings in Games 4 and 5. The Red Wings were limited to one goal in each of those losses, but Monday's first-period barrage more than made up for it.

Henrik Zetterberg finished the Wings' scoring, wristing in a short-handed goal early in the second.

Drake's first-period goal was his first of these playoffs. The Cup finals will also be a first for the 16-year veteran forward, who broke into the league with the Wings in 1992.

"Well, it's a huge thrill for me to get a chance to play in the Stanley Cup," he said. "I've never even gotten close to having an opportunity. Just real grateful. Play for a great team, great organization. Couldn't be more thankful right now than I am."

THREE STARS

DALLAS DRAKE — HENRIK ZETTERBERG — KRIS DRAPER

DETROIT RED WINGS
THE PLAYOFFS

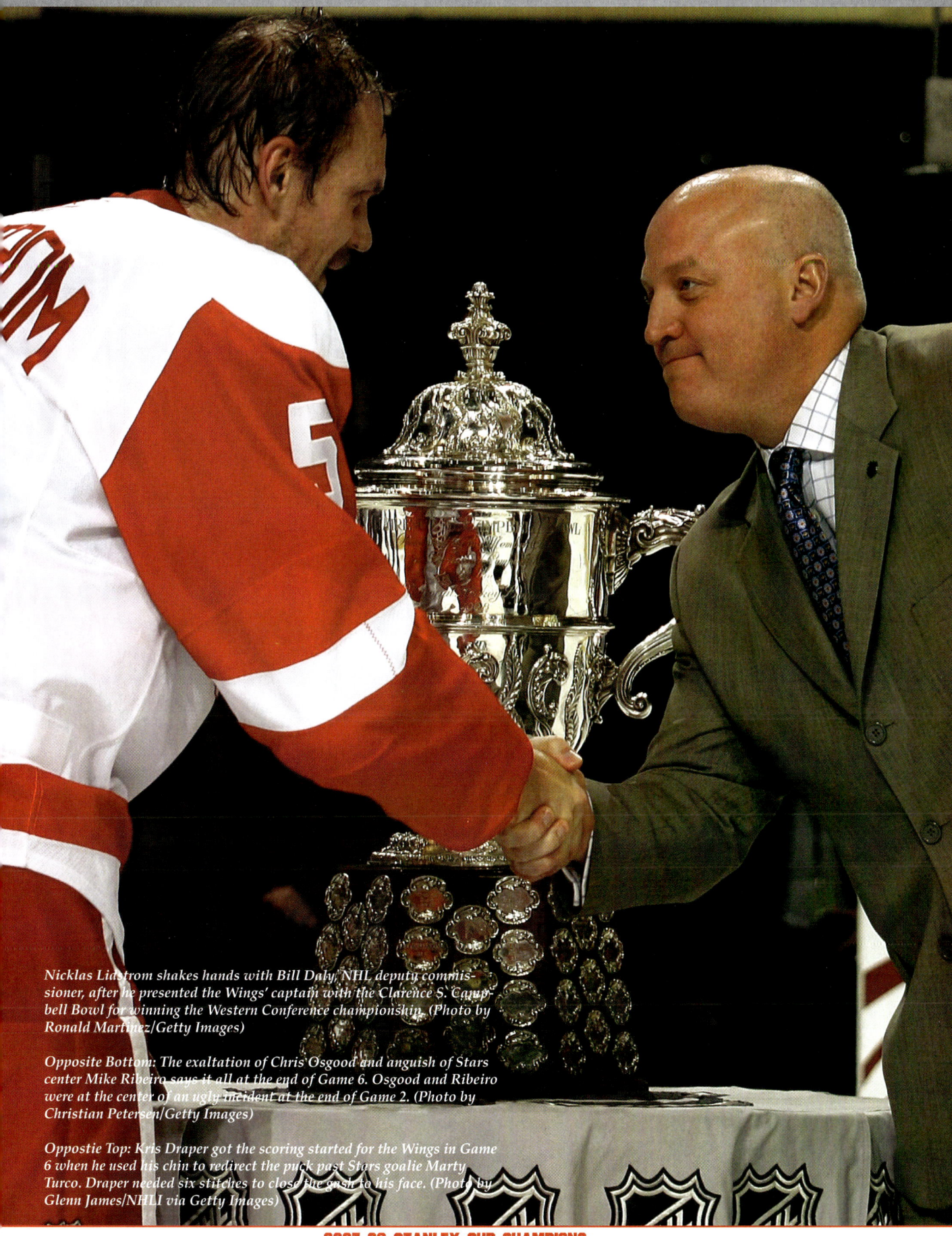

Nicklas Lidstrom shakes hands with Bill Daly, NHL deputy commissioner, after he presented the Wings' captain with the Clarence S. Campbell Bowl for winning the Western Conference championship. (Photo by Ronald Martinez/Getty Images)

Opposite Bottom: The exaltation of Chris Osgood and anguish of Stars center Mike Ribeiro says it all at the end of Game 6. Osgood and Ribeiro were at the center of an ugly incident at the end of Game 2. (Photo by Christian Petersen/Getty Images)

Oppostie Top: Kris Draper got the scoring started for the Wings in Game 6 when he used his chin to redirect the puck past Stars goalie Marty Turco. Draper needed six stitches to close the gash to his face. (Photo by Glenn James/NHLI via Getty Images)

2007-08 STANLEY CUP CHAMPIONS

2007-2008 THE CUP

THE STANLEY CUP

 VS.

PITTSBURGH 0   DETROIT 4

GAME 1 - MAY 24, 2008

Sammy's deuce paces Wings in Cup opener

By Derek Gluth

DETROIT -- All the talk coming into Game 1 of the Stanley Cup finals was about the big four – Pittsbugh's Sidney Crosby and Evgeni Malkin, and Red Wings' Henrik Zetterberg and Pavel Datsyuk.

Yet, after the game, the talk shifted to an unlikely scorer, Mikael Samuelsson. A wrap around goal and a rebound past Marc-Andre Fleury gave Samuelsson two unassisted goals, and helped lift the Red Wings to a 4-0 win and a 1-0 series edge.

"They turned the puck over at the red line, and I saw – the first one, they were out there, like, 30, 40 seconds," Samuelsson said. "I just took a shot at it. They went to the net; I couldn't really cut in front, so I had to go behind. I guess the goalie committed to me a little bit, so I took a chance to throw it at the net, and it went in."

For the Penguins, they realize that the focus can't be solely on the Wings' EuroTwins, but some acknowledge that things happen during a game.

"I think that those things happen, they have a good team, they have some depth, and you have to be aware of everyone," said Pens defenseman Hal Gill, who was on the ice for both Samuelsson goals.

Samuelsson seemed to be at the right place at the right time.

After a disallowed Red Wings' goal in the first period, both teams were looking to take advantage and score first, but it was Samuelsson -- the only player in this series to have played for both teams -- who put the Wings on top.

The goals proved to be the game-winner in Chris Osgood's second shutout of the postseason.

The second line scoring seemed to capitalize on Pittsburgh's mistakes.

"Bad decision with the puck; bad change," said Pittsburgh head coach Michel Therrien. "Those are mental mistakes against a team like the Red Wings. You can't do those type of mistakes."

THREE STARS

MIKAEL SAMUELSSON — CHRIS OSGOOD — DAN CLEARY
DETROIT RED WINGS

2007-08 STANLEY CUP CHAMPIONS

DETROIT RED WINGS
THE STANLEY CUP

Kris Draper celebrates the moment after Samuelsson's second goal gave the Wings a 2-0 lead in Game 1.

Opposite Top: Mikael Samuelsson is pumped, Below: The Red Wings are fired up after Mikael Samuelsson (not pictured) put Detroit up, 1-0 with his second-period wraparound goal. (Photo by Bruce Bennett/Getty Images)

Opposite Bottom: Chris Osgood wasn't overworked in Game 1, but he stopped all 19 shots that he faced, including this offering from Sidney Crosby. (Photo by Dave Sandford/Getty Images)

2007-08 STANLEY CUP CHAMPIONS

THE STANLEY CUP

GAME 2 - MAY 26, 2008

Oz–Good as it gets for the Wings

By Michael Caples

 vs.

PITTSBURGH 0   DETROIT 3

DETROIT -- For two straight games, Chris Osgood has been spectacular at shutting down the powerful offensive attack of the Pittsburgh Penguins.

But the veteran goalie's second performance wasn't without controversy.

Along the way, Osgood drew a pair of interference penalties on the Pens' Ryan Malone and Petr Sykora, the second leading to a few roughing infractions in the Detroit corner.

"I'll tell you something," Pittsburgh coach Michel Therrien said, "I reviewed those plays. He's a good actor. He goes to players, and he's diving. Took away our power play."

Pens center Maxime Talbot pointed out that it wasn't the first time Osgood fell to the ice on a questionable play. In Game 2 of the Western Conference final, Dallas forward Mike Ribeiro swung his stick and knocked over the Red Wings' goalie.

"I don't think he got pushed really hard out there," Talbot said. "He did the same thing against Ribeiro. If he wants to do that, that's a shame. We're not playing soccer."

Questionable calls or not, Osgood got the job done once again.

Perhaps it's a case of soar grapes on the Pens' part sense they're heading home for Wednesday's Game 2, down 2-0 in the series.

Teams that have swept their first two games at home in the Stanley Cup finals have a 30-1 record of spending the summer with the Cup.

Osgood's back-to-back shutouts mark the fifth time a Red Wings' goalie has turned the trick in the Cup finals. The others were Terry Sawchuk (1952), Harry Lumley (1945), John Mowers (1943), and Earl Robertson (1937) with all four eventually leading Detroit to Cup titles in those years.

"I don't know, I don't like bragging about myself very much," Osgood said. "I played some good games in my career. But I feel pretty good about myself right now."

Osgood only faced six shots in the first period, but those six saves may have been bigger than all 16 he made afterwards. It took Pittsburgh 12 minutes to register a shot, but when they came storming out on their first power play, the Detroit netminder was ready.

"He's been there the last two games," Tomas Holmstrom said. "He seems like he's been just so focused, getting rebounds, if they get rebounds we have the 'D' there."

Still the Pens labored the point that Osgood should be held accountable for diving.

"I would say he went down pretty easily there," Sidney Crosby said. "And I mean, he's trying to draw a penalty. But I think everyone has to be held accountable if that's a forward and they go down. A ref is calling a penalty if it's obvious. Why not call the same for a goaltender?"

THREE STARS

CHRIS OSGOOD   VALTTERI FILPPULA   BRAD STUART
DETROIT RED WINGS

2007-08 STANLEY CUP CHAMPIONS

THE STANLEY CUP

A diving Valtteri Filppula sneaks a peek at the puck as it floats past Marc-Andre Fleury in the third period of Game 2.

Left: A bird's eye view of Filppula's highlight reel goal. There was a delayed penalty on Pens defenseman Kris Letang, who tripped Filppula before the Wings' forward managed to get off his remarkable shot. (Photo by Dave Sandford/Getty Images)

Right: Yet another angle. (Photo by Claus Andersen/Getty Images)

Opposite Page: Osgood stops one of Sidney Crosby's six shots in Game 2. The Wings set a Cup finals record by starting the series with seven unanswered goals. (Photo by Jim McIsaac/Getty Images)

2007-08 STANLEY CUP CHAMPIONS

THE STANLEY CUP

 VS.

PITTSBURGH 3   **DETROIT 2**

GAME 3 – MAY 28, 2008
Pens thrive in friendly confines

By Lindsey Ungar

PITTSBURGH — Back at Mellon Arena, and back in business.

All the Penguins needed were 17,132 fans drenched in white from head to toe, swinging towels overhead.

"Every time you get a hit the fans go crazy," said Pens forward Adam Hall, who scored the game-winning goal. "And it just gives everyone on your team a boost. Every time you get a shot or goal, or every time the other team kinda trips up a little bit, the crowd's going nuts for a penalty call. It definitely helps us that's for sure."

The crowd stopped momentarily to breathe between chants of "Let's Go Pens!" and "Gary, Gary!" for fan favorite Gary Roberts.

But only a moment.

They were busy getting up and down for standing ovations, including one that lasted almost an entire commercial break after Brooks Orpik had four hits in a single shift in the third period.

"They love it here," defenseman Hal Gill said of the whiteout crowd. "They love the physical play. And that's what they want to see from their team. We had some guys that stepped up. And that shift by Orpik was one of the best I've ever seen. That's tough to do — to play at that level for that long. And he did. And they should be chanting his name."

It all started after the miracle happened — Sidney Crosby scored the Penguins' first goal of the series, ending goaltender Chris Osgood's personal shutout streak of more than 155-minutes.

The arena erupted in a deafening sigh of relief.

"You're like OK, now we're gonna win," forward Maxime Talbot said. "That's what we were telling each other. You know we get one, we're gonna roll out of that. And that's what happened."

The Pens fired five straight shots on Osgood to close the first.

Even the Penguins' mascot, Iceberg, seemed pretty excited — during the first intermission the large stuffed penguin cartwheeled onto the ice.

Pittsburgh carried over that play to the middle frame when Crosby added his second of the night, eliciting more reaction from the crowd.

The Mellon faithful heckled Osgood with rhythmic chants of "Oz-zie! Oz-zie!" And not the friendly kind Osgood receives at Joe Louis Arena. These were the drawn out, our-team-is-back-in-the-series type.

Johan Franzen's goal at 14:48 of the second cut the Penguins' lead in half. But the crowd didn't falter. And neither did the Penguins, who went on to a 3-2 victory in Game 3. They haven't lost at Mellon since Feb. 24, winning 17 straight contests.

"There was no panic with our club," Pittsburgh coach Michel Therrien said. "This has been three months we haven't lost a game here."

THREE STARS

SIDNEY CROSBY — PITTSBURGH PENGUINS   VALTTERI FILPPULA — DETROIT RED WINGS   MARIAN HOSSA — PITTSBURGH PENGUINS

DETROIT RED WINGS
THE STANLEY CUP

Opposite Bottom: Gary Roberts (10) and Tomas Holmstrom add to the confusion in front of the Penguins' net with this first-period collision in Game 3. (Photo by Jamie Sabau/Getty Images)

Opposite Top: Dallas Drake drives Penguins right wing Pascal Dupuis into the corner during a hard-hitting Game 3 at Mellon Arena. (Photo by Bruce Bennett/Getty Images)

After being shutout in two straight games, the Penguins finally scored on Chris Osgood. Here Sidney Crosby (87) celebrates his goal with teammate Jarkko Ruutu. (Photo by Gregory Shamus/Getty Images)

2007-08 STANLEY CUP CHAMPIONS

THE STANLEY CUP

 VS.

PITTSBURGH 1   DETROIT 2

GAME 4 - MAY 31, 2008

Osgood sees the Wings to 3-1 series lead

By Lindsey Ungar

PITTSBURGH — Chris Osgood made his case for the playoff MVP award, looking nothing short of magnificent in Game 4 of the Stanley Cup finals Saturday.

Kris Draper summed up Osgood's performance in the Wings' 2-1 win over the Penguins in one word: "Unbelievable."

With the Wings clinging to a one-goal lead, Osgood saved his best for the third period. But even on Pittsburgh's two-man advantage midway through the period, he was unflappable.

Evgeni Malkin's shot appeared to go over the goal line just as the final power play ended. The goal judge was fooled, while the crowd stood and cheered as the red light flashed for a second.

Osgood wasn't going to let the chance to possibly clinching the Stanley Cup in Game 5 at Joe Louis Arena slip away.

"Not just on that 5-on-3, but throughout the whole game I thought he made some key saves," captain Nicklas Lidstrom said. "He got the rebounds too. And on the 5-on-3, I thought he made two or three huge saves for us. He had point blank chances. … He really carried the game for us."

Osgood was solid throughout, and was certainly spectacular in the second when he was called upon to make consecutive Conn Smythe Trophy-worthy stops on Sidney Crosby, Pascal Dupuis and Marian Hossa with just over six minutes left in the middle frame.

Sure, Osgood can't get all the credit for the late kill or holding Pittsburgh to one goal, but he got plenty of recognition from the Penguins.

"They've had one of the best PK's in the regular-season, so as much as you want to point fingers at our guys, they gotta give them credit for what they're doing," Pens defenseman Brooks Orpik said. "Osgood's seeing the puck pretty well, and for the most part in the series, he makes saves on challenges, those guys do a great job of taking care of guys' sticks and second chances."

Since taking over for Dominik Hasek in Game 4 of the opening round against Nashville, Osgood has lost just three times.

No goofy goals. No crazy rebounds. No flashy saves.

Just the best goals-against average (1.45) and save percentage (.936) in the playoffs. And three shutouts.

THREE STARS

NICKLAS LIDSTROM
DETROIT RED WINGS

CHRIS OSGOOD
DETROIT RED WINGS

MARIAN HOSSA
PITTSBURGH PENGUINS

DETROIT RED WINGS
THE STANLEY CUP

Opposite Top: Chris Osgood makes one of his 22 saves in Game 4. (Photo by Gregory Shamus/Getty Images)

Opposite Bottom: Sidney Crosby is stymied by Henrik Zetterberg's backcheck, while Osgood reaches for the loose puck on the Penguins' 5-on-3 man advantage in the third period. (Photo by Gregory Shamus/Getty Images)

Bottom: Brian Rafalski and the Wings bottled up Sidney Crosby in Game 4, holding the young superstar pointless for the third time in the series. (Photo by Joseph Sargent/Getty Images)

Hudler celebrates his eventual game-winning goal in the third period of Game 4. (Photo by Jim McIsaac/Getty Images)

2007-08 STANLEY CUP CHAMPIONS

THE STANLEY CUP

GAME 5 - JUNE 2, 2008

Penguins live for another day

 VS.

PITTSBURGH 4   **DETROIT 3**

By Michael Caples

DETROIT -- Clinching at home continues to be a problem for the Red Wings, who failed to wrap up the Stanley Cup at Joe Louis Arena in Game 5 -- the second longest game in Red Wings' Cup finals history.

Pittsburgh right wing Petr Sykora scored at the 10:03 mark of the third overtime to send the series back to the Steel City for Game 6.

The Red Wings mounted a third period comeback on goals by Pavel Datsyuk and Brian Rafalski, but it wasn't enough to hold off the Penguins, who forced overtime with Maxime Talbot's goal with 35-seconds left in regulation.

"You know, we really battled our way back," said coach Mike Babcock, who's team trailed 2-0 after the first period. "We had every opportunity. And we had it twice, one at the red line and one on the half wall. And we didn't get it deep, and we never got it out. In the end, they scored, and we never scored on our chances in overtime."

The Red Wings have not clinched a playoff series at Joe Louis Arena since they captured the Stanley Cup on home ice in 2002.

"Well, I mean, I thought we had every opportunity to win the game, obviously," Babcock said. "I thought we were really nervous. We never made a play in the first period, for whatever reason. And whether that's focusing on outcome rather than just process and doing what you always do."

Defenseman Niklas Kronwall said the Wings never underestimated the Penguins.

"No one thought they were out of it," Kronwall said. "Obviously they battled hard. They played well and (Marc-Andre) Fleury in particular had a good game."

The Red Wings out-shot Pittsburgh, 58-32, but with Jiri Hudler in the box serving a four-minute high sticking call, Sykora beat goalie Chris Osgood from the top of the right circle. The winger took a feed from Evgeni Malkin, and ripped a shot over Osgood's left shoulder.

THREE STARS

MARC-ANDRE FLEURY — PITTSBURGH PENGUINS
PETR SYKORA — PITTSBURGH PENGUINS
HENRIK ZETTERBERG — DETROIT RED WINGS

DETROIT RED WINGS

THE STANLEY CUP

Pens forward Ryan Malone celebrates Petr Sykora's game-winner in triple overtime to the chagrin of the Red Wings, including Nicklas Lidstrom, Andreas Lilja (3) and Chris Osgood (30). (Photo by Christian Petersen/Getty Images)

Opposite bottom: Despite being tripped by Evgeni Malkin (71), Pavel Datsyuk beats goalie Marc-Andre Fleury in the third period of Game 5. Unfortunately, the puck clanked off the crossbar. (Photo by Dave Sandford/Getty Images)

Opposite Top: Darren Helm delivers one of his six hits – victimizing Pens defenseman Ryan Whitney – in six-minutes of ice-time during regulation in Game 5.

2007-08 STANLEY CUP CHAMPIONS

THE STANLEY CUP

GAME 6 - JUNE 4, 2008

Hometown Rafalski seals Hockeytown deal

PITTSBURGH 2   DETROIT 3

By Michael Caples

PITTSBURGH -- All it took was a little magic from the hometown kid.

Brian Rafalski, who grew up minutes from Joe Louis Arena in suburban Dearborn, thought he had the Stanley Cup-clinching goal in Game 5. To make up for it, he scored right out of the gate in Game 6.

Rafalski's fourth goal of the playoffs gave the Red Wings the all-important first goal in Game 6. Taking a pass from Henrik Zetterberg, he skated it in towards the Penguins goal, and fired a wrist shot into the back of the net.

Valtteri Filppula scored in the second, and Zetterberg scored in the third as the Red Wings marched to a 3-2 victory en route to their fourth Stanley Cup title in 11 years.

Rafalski learned the game on youth teams at Melvindale's local ice arena. He spent his teen years at Southfield Christian High School, and some years later, he found his way back home, just in time to win a Stanley Cup with his hometown team.

The 34-year-old took a round-about way to get to this moment. Having not been drafted, the University of Wisconsin graduate traveled to Europe, where he played a season in Sweden and four in Finland. New Jersey signed Rafalski in 1999, and he totaled five goals and 27 assists in his first season. In his seven seasons with the Devils, the right-handed defenseman accumulated 44 goals and 267 assists with an astounding plus-100 rating. Along the way, his name was engraved on the Stanley Cup – twice, in 2000 and 2002.

Rafalski had 13 goals and 42 assists in the regular-season, finished second in playoff scoring amongst defensemen with 14 points, one behind teammate Niklas Kronwall.

THREE STARS

HENRIK ZETTERBERG — DETROIT RED WINGS
BRIAN RAFALSKI — DETROIT RED WINGS
EVGENI MALKIN — PITTSBURGH PENGUINS

2007-08 STANLEY CUP CHAMPIONS

THE STANLEY CUP

Pittsburgh's Adam Hall can't prevent Henrik Zetterberg from making a pass to Brian Rafalski, who fired a shot into the Pens' net for a 1-0 lead. (Photo by Dave Sandford/Getty Images)

Opposite Bottom: Zetterberg zips into the offensive zone during the second period, leaving Pens forward Marian Hossa in his wake. (Photo by Gregory Shamus/Getty Images)

Opposite Top: Osgood, who made 20 saves in the game, stops Pens forward Gary Roberts on this chance in the third period.

2007-08 STANLEY CUP CHAMPIONS

DETROIT RED WINGS
THE STANLEY CUP

In the waning milliseconds of Game 6, Chris Osgood dives for a loose puck, dashing the Penguins' hopes of forcing a Game 7 back in Detroit. Osgood was spectacular during the finals, even shutting out Pittsburgh in the first two games. (Photo by Dave Sandford/Getty Images)

2007-08 STANLEY CUP CHAMPIONS

Zetterberg, a real Conn artist

By Lindsey Ungar

PITTSBURGH — Henrik Zetterberg is following in Nicklas Lidstrom's footsteps.

And that can only be a great thing for the Red Wings, who wrapped up their fourth Stanley Cup in 11 seasons.

Zetterberg joined Lidstrom as the only European-born players to win the Conn Smythe Trophy as the playoff's most valuable player.

In the Cup-clincher, Zetterberg delivered the final blow to the Penguins when his wrist shot trickled through the legs of goalie Marc-Andre Fleury at 7:36 of the third period.

Zetterberg's tremendous two-way play silenced the Pens' dreams of a miracle comeback. His third-period goal put the Pens in a two-goal hole, which eventually led to a 3-2 Red Wings' victory. He also assisted on Brian Rafalski's goal, and again was stellar in his backchecking role, clearing Pittsburgh's best chance on a long 5-on-3 in the first period.

Zetterberg's 27 points set a new franchise postseason record, surpassing Sergei Fedorov and Steve Yzerman. And that was while shutting down the top guns from Pittsburgh, Dallas and Nashville.

"He's meant a great deal to our team," defenseman Niklas Kronwall said. "I think everybody starts to see that. He's our best offensive guy, while at the same time our best defensive guy, he plays all situations. And we're lucky to have him. There's not a lot of guys like him in the league."

In the end, a case could have been made for Lidstrom, Chris Osgood, or even Johan Franzen. There was no clear-cut winner on a team where every skater got at least a point in the postseason.

But while those players have a specialty, Zetterberg is the all-around superstar.

"One of the best two-way players I've ever seen," general manager Ken Holland said. "When your top player is your top defensive player, and he can play in all different types of situations — power play, penalty kill, on a regular shift — you're going to have a good team."

Zetterberg made his team great this postseason. He was consistent, with a nine-game point streak midway through the postseason. And he saved his best for last — none better than killing almost the entire 5-on-3 late in Game 3.

NBC broadcaster Doc Emrick called it a "Conn-Smythe worthy shift."

And it was. That shift tipped the series to Detroit — for good. The Wings weren't going to blow three chances to win the Cup.

Zetterberg blocked a Sergei Gonchar point shot, prevented Sidney Crosby from a doorstep dump-in, and stole the puck away from Evgeni Malkin to get a solid scoring chance.

That was the only shot of the 5-on-3, as Pittsburgh fired blanks in the most important 1:26 minutes of the season — courtesy of the man know throughout Hockeytown as Z.

Offense, defense? There's never been a line to cross for Zetterberg, a rare offensive superstar that kills penalties for kicks. And he led the playoffs in shorthand points (five) for some extra pizzazz. He was a plus-16 — best in the postseason and a testament to his diverse game.

"A lot of players don't get it until later on in their career," said former Detroit coach Scotty Bowman, who gets credit for morphing Yzerman into a double threat.

Zetterberg's got it. And he's 27-years-old, playing just his fifth NHL season.

Hard to believe he was passed over 209 times before being selected by the Red Wings in the seventh round of the 1999 draft.

Now, he's a Conn Smythe and Stanley Cup winner, and likely a Selke winner, too.

Zetterberg's got everything now. But it's only the beginning.

DETROIT RED WINGS
THE STANLEY CUP

2007-08 STANLEY CUP CHAMPIONS

DETROIT RED WINGS
THE STANLEY CUP

2007-08 STANLEY CUP CHAMPIONS

DETROIT RED WINGS
THE STANLEY CUP

2007-08 STANLEY CUP CHAMPIONS

DETROIT RED WINGS
THE STANLEY CUP

2007-08 STANLEY CUP CHAMPIONS

DETROIT RED WINGS
THE FANS

Thanks for the support

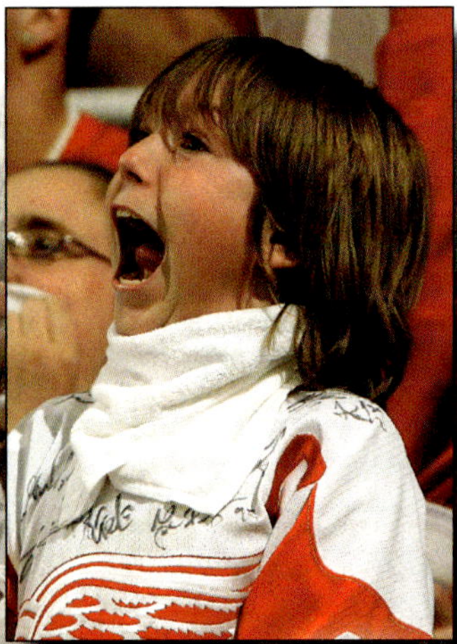

2007-08 STANLEY CUP CHAMPIONS